Teen Smoking
Understanding the Risk

Daniel McMillan

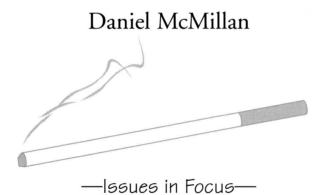

—Issues in Focus—

Enslow Publishers, Inc.

44 Fadem Road	PO Box 38
Box 699	Aldershot
Springfield, NJ 07081	Hants GU12 6BP
USA	UK

Library of Congress Cataloging-in-Publication Data

McMillan, Daniel.
    Teen smoking : understanding the risk / Daniel McMillan.
        p.   cm. — (Issues in focus)
    Includes bibliographical references and index.
    Summary: Focuses on the health risks associated with tobacco use, tactics
employed by tobacco manufacturers, social consequences of smoking, prevention
efforts, and treatment options.
    ISBN 0-89490-722-0
    1. Teenagers—Tobacco use—United States—Juvenile literature. 2. Smoking—
United States—Juvenile literature. 3. Tobacco habit—United States—Juvenile
literature. [1. Tobacco habit. 2. Smoking.] I. Title. II. Series: Issues in focus
(Hillside, N.J.)
HV5745.M353   1998
362.29'6'0835—dc20   96-36323
                                                              CIP
                                                              AC

10 9 8 7 6 5 4 3

Illustration Credits: Kevin Eans, p. 45; Author's Personal Collection, pp. 8,
27, 47; © Corel Corporation, pp. 10, 20, 33, 51, 53, 62, 66, 79, 88; Food
and Drug Administration, p. 40.

Cover Credit: Enslow Publishers, Inc.

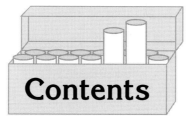

Contents

1

The Power of Tobacco

Seated in the food court of a busy shopping mall, a young girl lights up. At first, she appears relaxed and confident as she tilts her neck and sends a narrow column of smoke overhead. Temporarily removed from the hurried pace of the other shoppers, she seems content to enjoy a cigarette, drink a soda, and sit in the warm sunlight that streams down from an overhead skylight. But the period of calm is brief.

"I'm trying to smoke two cigarettes quick. Before my mom picks me up," she explains. "She'll be here any minute. I think she knows I smoke, but she's never really confronted me about it. And this is not the day I want her to confront me, either."

At the age of fifteen, she has been smoking for a year and a half. She likes smoking, but plans to quit when she gets older—seventeen or eighteen would be a good age to drop the habit, she thinks. It's a drag to always be on edge about getting caught, she says, especially when it's really no big deal to smoke just a few cigarettes a day.

"I know it's supposed to be bad for you, but it's not like I'm addicted or anything. I just like it, that's all. I'll quit when I'm ready. No big deal."

On the surface, at least, smoking cigarettes and other types of tobacco use may seem like no big deal. For the most part, the dangers are not immediately apparent—it is not as if people die after smoking one or two cigarettes, or even after one or two packs of cigarettes. Furthermore, plenty of people smoke and chew tobacco, some of them for years and years, without it seeming to cause any serious problems.

It is clear, though, that tobacco use is actually one of the most serious threats to good health and well-being. Years of scientific research by scores of health professionals in the United States and other nations have confirmed the many connections to cancer, heart disease, and other illnesses. Even the manufacturers of tobacco, after many years of denying the harmful health consequences associated with the use of their products, now assert that smokers knowingly accept the risks of tobacco use.

Numbers of Deaths

The figures regarding the health effects of tobacco use are stark and clear. The federal Centers for Disease Control and Prevention (CDC) estimates that tobacco use kills more than eight thousand Americans each week—more than four hundred thousand each year.[1]

Here is another way of looking at the numbers: What would you think if every single day of the year the newspapers and television news informed you that two jumbo jets packed with passengers had crashed, killing everyone on board? Would you be looking forward to your next plane ride? Probably not. As a matter of fact, you might even be a little hesitant to leave your home for fear of falling debris from airplane crashes. Now consider this: The number of people who would die in a year in those two-a-day airplane disasters would be less than the number of people who *actually* die every year from smoking-related diseases.

This phenomenal legacy of death is the result of a habit that controls the lives of more than 46 million people in this country. Recent estimates count about 24 million men and 22 million women in the United States as smokers. Estimates for numbers of teenagers smoking come in at about 3 million, nearly evenly divided between boys and girls.[2]

The statistics and the stories go on and on, each telling the same tale in different words: Smoking is the leading cause of preventable illness and premature death in the United States today. Startling though they are, however, the facts and figures about tobacco-related disease and death somehow fail to convey the sense of imminent peril that one might normally consider appropriate for a product that is directly linked to the deaths of more than four hundred thousand people. In a dark and mysterious way, the grim statistics seem to merely dangle there, a sort of backdrop for a stage where the story of tobacco continues to play itself out, generation after generation after generation.

To fully appreciate the story of tobacco, and perhaps to understand its widespread use despite the obvious health consequences, it is helpful to understand some of the key themes of the tale. First and foremost, tobacco is

Cigarette advertising has relied heavily on recognizable images from popular culture, including television actors. This example features stars from the television series *Gunsmoke*.

a legal product and it is openly sold and advertised as such in every state. Unlike a lot of other products that are considered lethal and addictive, tobacco has been granted special legal status in the United States, exempt from many laws designed to protect consumer health and safety.

Furthermore, tobacco has played an important role in the nation's past and, as an industry, it continues to enjoy enormous clout even today. Ongoing government subsidies to tobacco farmers (about $50 million annually) and generous tax breaks for tobacco manufacturers, despite the well-known health hazards of their product, illustrate the enduring power and influence of this commodity.

Another important feature of the tobacco story is the remarkably successful marketing of the product. Over many years, an array of skillful advertising and promotional tactics—the clever use of doctors, glamorous models, and humorous cartoon figures in advertisements; the inclusion of cigarettes in the rations provided to Americans serving in the armed forces; the glitzy catalogs full of attractive merchandise that can be earned by purchasing cigarettes—have helped to build a large and loyal consumer base for tobacco products.

Its legal status, its history, and an effective marketing strategy have served tobacco well and, until very recently, helped overshadow the negative health consequences of tobacco use. In rather dramatic fashion, however, the tide appears to be turning against the industry and its products—and, in some cases, even against smokers themselves. Motivated largely by growing concern for the health of nonsmokers exposed to "secondhand smoke," a broad social movement against smoking has been gaining momentum in the United States.

Many schools, offices, and public facilities have implemented antismoking policies, some strict government regulations have come into effect, and even stricter rules are on the horizon. On August 22, 1996, President Bill Clinton announced tough new measures to outlaw cigarette ads pitched at kids and to ban tobacco vending machines in areas frequented by minors. And in recent years, the tobacco manufacturers have been hit with huge lawsuits that could potentially force some of them out of business.

This onslaught against the tobacco industry set the stage for a landmark $368.5 billion settlement proposal in the summer of 1997 between the major U.S. tobacco companies and the attorneys-general of forty U.S. states. At the time of this book's publication, the details of the proposed settlement were still under review by the White

President Bill Clinton took a stand against cigarette advertisements aimed at young people. He enacted measures that banned tobacco vending machines in areas frequented by minors.

House and Congress, as well as influential public health groups. Acceptance by each of these parties is required before the deal can be implemented, a process that could take months or even years. It is also possible that the proposed deal could fall apart without any changes being implemented.

If enacted, however, some of the settlement's main provisions include:

- The tobacco industry would have to pay $50 billion over twenty-five years to fund health care for uninsured children and future health programs.

- The industry would have to spend $500 million on antismoking messages geared toward young people. If reduction in teenage smoking does not meet specified targets, the industry would face additional fines.

- Warning labels on cigarette packages would become much larger and the language would be much stronger. For example, new warnings might state: "Smoking can kill you," or "Cigarettes are addictive."

- Advertising and marketing targeted at young people, including Joe Camal and Marlboro Man campaigns, would end. Billboard advertising would be prohibited. Tobacco companies could no longer sponsor sporting events or concerts, give away products with cigarette brand names or logos, or place their products in movies or on television.

- Smoking in most public places would be banned.

- In return for these and other industry concessions, state lawsuits seeking repayment from Medicaid expenses would end and no more class-action lawsuits could be filed by smokers seeking punitive damages.[3]

11

Smoking, once considered glamorous and chic, has quite literally been thrown out of the house—lighting up is now mostly an outdoor activity, and if these new provisions are enacted, it will be prohibited even there.

Considering its well-documented health effects and the strong social movement against its use, perhaps the most amazing feature of the tobacco story is, as noted earlier, the degree to which it is still overlooked as a serious danger by so many people, especially young people. But, like any good mystery story, the tale of tobacco in the United States is complicated and intriguing. With a fascinating plot and a unique cast of characters, the tobacco story has enjoyed a long run and huge audience appeal. This story and its continuing appeal shall be explored in this book.

Readers of this book should not only develop a clear understanding of the health risks associated with tobacco use, but should also learn about some important related issues, including:

- the subtle and sophisticated tactics employed by tobacco manufacturers to encourage the use of their products;

- the social consequences of smoking, including sometimes divisive debates over smoking policies and the provision of health care to smokers;

- various strategies designed to prevent the start of tobacco use, especially among young people; and

- the difficult process of ending the tobacco use habit.

In 1993, the tobacco industry spent $6.2 billion on advertising and promoting cigarettes and smokeless tobacco. Tobacco advertising expenditures have increased more than 1,500 percent between 1970 (the year before television and radio advertising was banned) and 1992.[1]

—Food and Drug Administration

2

Why People Smoke

On the surface, at least, the makers and marketers of tobacco products appear to be waging an uphill battle. Most people now know that the use of cigarettes and other tobacco products is hazardous to their health and, in case they ever forget, a multitude of antismoking forces stand ready to remind them of the perils.

One indication of the hostile attitude facing tobacco is a statement former U.S. Surgeon General Joycelyn Elders made: "I'm sure that if cigarettes were introduced today, with all that we know about them, we would never allow them to be sold."[2]

This brief statement says a great deal. It refers directly to the current dim view of tobacco taken by the public health community and indirectly to the previous success that tobacco manufacturers have enjoyed in selling their product in this country. But, perhaps most importantly, it reveals that tobacco use in the United States is a part of this nation's history and culture. It is certainly not a new phenomenon.

To fully understand and appreciate the current environment surrounding tobacco, it is important to view the issue in its historical context. Understanding some of these historical realities provides a useful framework when trying to comprehend the continuing appeal of a product that is widely recognized to be both addictive and lethal.

From the standpoint of the mid-1990s, tobacco as a consumer product is at the center of some terrific paradoxes, or contradicting ideas. Perhaps the most obvious paradox is that, despite overwhelming evidence of the harmful effects of smoking and widespread public acceptance of such evidence, cigarettes continue to claim the lives of more than four hundred thousand people each year. Smoking is, by far, the leading cause of preventable illness and premature death in our society.[3] Another important paradox concerns young Americans. While smoking rates in the general population have been in a relatively steady decline for more than a generation, the percentage of young smokers has been increasing in recent years.

For the modern observer of the tobacco issue, it is important to recognize that such paradoxes have not emerged in our society in the same fashion that Dorothy made her famous appearance in the Land of Oz. Rather, they are the logical consequences of certain historical realities, deliberate efforts, and continuing public policies.

A Brief History

Leaving aside momentarily the many divisive issues that now surround tobacco, there can be little debate that this leafy member of the nightshade plant family has occupied a lofty and favored place on the stage of American history. Its growth and eventual dominance as a cash crop in many agricultural states, its successful marketing to consumers throughout the world, and its status as the financial underpinning of some of the most powerful multinational corporations and prominent philanthropic organizations all testify to the important position tobacco has long held in society.

Dating back to the colonial era and before, tobacco has played a central role in American history. In fact, tobacco played a large part in enabling European settlers to establish their first firm foothold in the New World. At Jamestown, Virginia, the first successful European settlement in North America, tobacco led the way. After enduring several years of poverty and hunger, the Jamestown settlers began to cultivate "Virginia leaf" tobacco in 1612. The proceeds from the sale of that tobacco to markets in Europe ensured the economic survival of Jamestown and thereby encouraged additional settlement ventures.

In the Americas, it was used as a barter item in transactions between Native Americans and the early settlers. Native Americans themselves had used tobacco for both ceremonial and recreational purposes, long before Europeans arrived.

Once established as a leading commercial crop in the eighteenth century, tobacco also influenced the development of the slave trade in North America. Large tobacco and cotton plantations in the middle Atlantic and southern regions were dependent on an abundance of cheap labor. As it became clear that European immigrants could not or would not fulfill this need, plantation owners turned to slave traders to provide laborers.

The invention of the cigarette-rolling machine in 1881 paved the way for the introduction of cigarettes into popular culture in the late nineteenth and early twentieth century. Mass marketing of cigarettes helped a handful of tobacco barons gain enormous wealth, and with it great power and influence. Even today, some of the nation's most recognizable institutions stand as enduring symbols of that power and influence: Duke University, for example, owes its name to James Buchanan Duke, founder of the American Tobacco Company, who donated tens of millions of dollars to the North Carolina university.

By the early 1950s, smoking in the United States enjoyed nearly universal acceptance and widespread social appeal. Tobacco products were used by the majority of men and a significant minority of women. Riding this wave of unchallenged popularity, tobacco companies earned enormous profits from their products, especially cigarettes.

The Turn in the Road

Seen against such a background of corporate power and social prestige, the more recent history of tobacco in the United States appears to be the cultural equivalent of a train wreck. The tobacco industry's strength was at its peak in this country in the 1950s and 1960s. Then, medical researchers issued the first of what would be a long stream of studies conclusively linking smoking with

16

lung cancer and other diseases. Since that time, the negative health associations tied to tobacco have continued to pile up.

Faced with information that threatened their favored position in the American lifestyle, the tobacco companies were not about to admit defeat and close down. They engaged in sophisticated advertising campaigns and tough legal tactics to defend their products against the increasingly damaging health findings. In addition, according to internal documents made public in 1994 and 1995, tobacco industry executives in the 1960s acted to suppress scientific evidence from their own research laboratories—evidence that showed cigarette smoking was a serious health risk and that nicotine, the active ingredient in tobacco, was addictive.[4]

The Surgeon General's Report

The 1964 release of U.S. Surgeon General Luther Terry's report on smoking was a watershed of sorts for both the public health community and the tobacco industry. It was the first widely publicized document from official sources to describe the link between smoking and lung cancer. Other government agencies soon followed the surgeon general's report with regulations that required health warnings on cigarette packaging and, eventually, banned cigarette advertising from radio and television.

From a public health standpoint, Americans' response to the message about the dangers of smoking has been quite positive. The number of cigarettes smoked per person in the United States never returned to levels seen before the release of the first surgeon general's report.[5] In addition, in the past thirty years, there has been a marked decline in the number of smokers in the United States— from about 40 percent of all adults in 1965 to about 25 percent today.

Today, however, despite declining use in the United States, the scope and influence of tobacco remains extensive. Industry-wide, it includes more than 40,000 manufacturing employees and 135,000 tobacco farmers.[6] Traditional tobacco giants Philip Morris and RJR Nabisco—now diversified conglomerates with business interests reaching far beyond cigarettes—are among the most elite corporations in the United States, worth billions of dollars.[7] While a sizable portion of the wealth generated by these companies is channeled to top corporate officials (Philip Morris's chief executive officer received total direct compensation of $7.8 million in 1994),[8] profits also benefit millions of Americans and others worldwide who hold tobacco stock or own mutual funds that invest in tobacco.

Tobacco Money

The modern tobacco industry has also used its economic strength to establish an influential presence in other arenas, including politics and the arts. A 1995 study conducted by the organization Common Cause found that tobacco interests contributed more than $16.6 million to federal political candidates or party committees in the previous decade.[9] Tobacco money has been spent liberally to influence politics at the state level, too. In California, for example, a university study estimated that the tobacco lobby contributed nearly $25 million in 1994 alone in an unsuccessful effort to win passage of Proposition 188, a statewide law that would have overturned many local tobacco-control measures.[10] In spite of this particular setback, critics argue that the tobacco industry's political investments have paid handsome dividends in terms of exemptions from the stricter laws on consumer product safety, product packaging, and hazardous and toxic substances that govern the use of other consumer products.

Substantial funding of high-profile arts organizations, including New York City's Lincoln Center and the Alvin Ailey Dance Theater, helps furbish the public image of the tobacco industry. For corporations that are otherwise routinely criticized for contributing only illness and death to society, the goodwill and leverage gained through this philanthropy is very welcome, indeed.

So, the lengthy story of tobacco leads now to the current circumstances: a politically charged environment in which powerful forces representing opposing views are locked in a high-stakes battle. The battle is being waged not only in courtrooms throughout the country, but in schoolyards, restaurants, office buildings, and any other place where people gather. All parties in the conflict claim to be fighting for principles that most Americans value— principles such as "freedom" and "individual rights."

The Conflict Over Smoking

On one side are individuals and organizations—many concerned with protecting and promoting good health— who wish to see greater restrictions and regulations placed on tobacco sale, promotion, and use. These parties have

The tobacco industry has provided substantial funding to many high-profile arts organizations.

generally applauded recent moves in our society to limit smoking.

On another side are individuals and organizations who wish to retain the opportunity to enjoy tobacco products. These parties have scoffed at many of the efforts to discourage smoking. Unhappy with increasing restrictions on smoking and perplexed by the spreading disdain for their habit, many smokers undoubtedly agree with the *Time* magazine headline that described them as "the one dysfunctional minority nobody cares about."[11]

Why Smoke?

Perhaps the most interesting aspect of the tobacco story is the continuing appeal of the product itself, despite its long list of negative associations. Given all that is now known about the serious health implications of tobacco use, and with society's attitudes shifting so dramatically against tobacco, it is fair to ask, "Why do nearly 50 million people in the United States continue to light up?" It's a question that millions of parents, teachers, health professionals, adolescents—and many smokers—ask. As one might expect, there are no easy answers.

It is difficult to imagine a consumer product on the market today that rivals the undesirable consequences associated with the regular use of tobacco: cancers of the lung, breast, mouth, pharynx, and esophagus; heart disease and stroke; severe respiratory problems, including pneumonia, chronic bronchitis, and emphysema; birth defects and reproductive disorders; stained teeth and fingernails; wrinkled skin; and bad breath. Then there is the thorny problem of addiction, which most experts say plagues the majority of tobacco consumers after only a relatively short period of regular usage. And because of the reported dangers of environmental tobacco smoke— the smoke exhaled by smokers and that given off by burning cigarettes, cigars, and pipes—adverse health effects are believed to extend to a great many nonsmokers as well.

Amazingly, in the face of this powerful lineup of unwanted health outcomes and the increased social pressure on smokers to kick the habit, tobacco products today are anything but hard to sell. In fact, American tobacco companies have experienced near-record profits in recent years.[12] Much of the growth in tobacco company profits is fueled by booming sales of U.S. cigarettes in overseas markets. In contrast to the chronic trade deficits that plague many other sectors of the U.S. economy, tobacco exports exceeded imports by a record $5.8 billion in 1994.[13] Also, according to the U.S. Department of Agriculture, cigarette production in the United States rose by 10 percent in 1994 to its second-highest level ever, and America's smokers puffed approximately 485 billion cigarettes.[14]

How might the continuing popularity of tobacco products be explained? Could it be that Americans just don't know the unpleasant facts about tobacco? Perhaps the message just has not been communicated effectively. Yet, a virtual landslide of information over the past thirty years argues against such a simple explanation. The 1964 U.S. surgeon general's report on the ill effects of smoking was followed by a torrent of scientific reports on tobacco, each further detailing harmful aspects of its use. The most important of these reports have been widely distributed to a mass audience eager for health information. Almost two generations of Americans have come of age in this era of easy access to information about smoking. Furthermore, it appears the message about the dangers of tobacco is accepted by vast majorities in the United States. A 1985 Gallup poll revealed a stunning 94 percent of Americans believed smoking was truly hazardous to health.[15]

At least among most adult populations, faulty communication or lack of information does not seem to be the problem. Even when confronted with easily remedied situations, most smokers appear unwilling or unable to take action to safeguard their health. A recent high-profile example of smokers' failure to respond to important health information came in the spring of 1995, when Philip Morris announced the recall of 8 billion cigarettes, including popular brands like Marlboro, Virginia Slims, and Merit. The company said the cigarettes were potentially tainted with a dangerous chemical that could cause smokers to experience dizziness and wheezing as well as eye, nose, and throat irritation. While there were widespread warnings in the media, and the company offered to provide free replacements for all returned cigarettes, most smokers greeted the recall with a collective yawn and smoked the cigarettes they had originally purchased.

This question of why people smoke is especially important to individuals involved in protecting people's health—doctors, nurses, public health officials, and other health care professionals. For many years, people in these professions have been the ones treating patients, conducting research, and analyzing statistics—all the while accumulating a vast arsenal of information about the harmful health effects of tobacco use.

As Surgeon General Antonia C. Novello stated in a report, a distressing gap remains between what is known about tobacco use and what health professionals seek to accomplish.

> We need no longer be mired in demonstrating the harmful effects of smoking. We have informed the public of these effects, and ongoing surveys demonstrate that many have acquired the knowledge. We must now provoke action based on that knowledge: abandonment of smoking by those who do; prevention of initiation by those who contemplate smoking; and regulation of the environment for everyone.[16]

To the immense frustration of most in the health field, the goal of provoking action based on knowledge, as Dr. Novello put it, continues to be elusive. Echoing the comments of Dr. Novello, two leading scientists involved in smoking research expressed frustration in a 1994 publication:

> Under the best of circumstances, knowledge brings about changes in behavior and public policy. . . . Decades of careful medical research have documented the hazards of smoking. Social scientists continue to investigate and define the factors that impede efforts to prevent the use of tobacco. We know that nicotine is an addictive substance and that our children are very vulnerable to this addiction. We know that smoking is the single greatest cause of death in the United States. Yet, we are still plagued by an entirely preventable problem . . . [17]

The continuing appeal of tobacco products is not easily combated. In trying to answer the question of why people smoke despite compelling evidence of its damaging effects, it is necessary to understand the many contributing factors, including:

- persuasive and well-financed marketing efforts by tobacco manufacturers;

- multiple social aspects that lead people, particularly youth, to experiment with cigarettes; and

- the reality of physical and psychological addiction.

Marketing

The tobacco industry's most important and visible marketing efforts involve two distinct activities: advertising and promotion. As the section below explains, these marketing activities are related, but they are not the same.

Tobacco companies spend around $6 billion per year advertising and promoting cigarettes.[18] While there is some debate about the intended effect of tobacco marketing efforts, the end result is indisputable. The tobacco companies' inventive, scientific, well-financed marketing techniques add up to millions of new smokers in the United States and around the world every year, many of whom remain lifetime users of cigarettes.

Like the history of tobacco itself, the annals of tobacco advertising are long and colorful. Since the early years of the twentieth century, cigarette manufacturers have employed positive imagery in their advertising, ranging from claims of better health to messages about beauty, increased popularity, fun, and independence.

25

Through the years, the tobacco companies have exhibited an uncanny ability to shift gears, moving from one marketing theme to another as different developments cast doubt on the safety of their products.

From the 1920s to the 1950s, health themes were used in the advertising of all the major cigarette makers in the United States. The ads were designed to portray smoking as perfectly safe, if not beneficial. Camel cigarettes were said to "increase your flow of energy." Lucky Strikes supposedly allowed "men to keep healthy and fit." The ads routinely depicted doctors and nurses enjoying a cigarette, as if to reassure consumers that even the people most concerned about good health were smoking.

As the tobacco companies' bogus health themes began to wilt under the heat of medical research, they shifted to messages touting the invention of filtered cigarettes and the "miraculous" safety and health protection these little tips provided.

The Marlboro Man. The most successful cigarette advertising campaign in history is Philip Morris's Marlboro Man, the rugged cowboy who has come to represent not only the Marlboro brand but also certain sentiments valued by many Americans; indeed, close to the very notion of what it means to be an American. For more than thirty years, the handsome Marlboro Man riding his horse across the wide-open Western range or relaxing beside a campfire at the end of a long, dusty day has conveyed a free-spirited attitude, a sense of independence and self-reliance, and most of all rugged masculinity. On the strength of that cowboy image— undeniably one of the most powerful and enduring icons

This 1940s-era cigarette advertisement stresses the "mildness" of the product. Notice the added appeal to health concerns with the tag, "More doctors smoke Camels than any other cigarette."

in the American imagination—Philip Morris has built Marlboro into the best-selling brand of cigarettes.

While the Marlboro Man certainly appeals to the masculine segment of the market, women have not been ignored by the tobacco industry. Beginning in 1928, the American Tobacco Company began pushing its Lucky Strike brand with the slogan "Reach for a Lucky Instead of a Sweet." The ads were targeted specifically to women and often featured popular celebrities of the day testifying that Lucky Strikes kept them thin and petite. That "thinness theme" was used again in the 1960s with the introduction of various "women's brands," such as Virginia Slims, and it continues even today with the many ads that feature attractive, slim, young female models. Even when a message about body shape and weight control is not plainly stated—and often it is—the effort to draw a connection between smoking and slimness is apparent.

Another, more recent, aspect of cigarette advertising is the use of humor or mockery. The Philip Morris brand Benson & Hedges has been at the forefront of this movement with its ads that depict smokers perched in precarious locations—atop the Statue of Liberty or on the ledges of high-rise office buildings—in pursuit of a place to smoke in peace. Like all sophisticated advertisements, the Benson & Hedges ads convey multiple messages: They poke fun at increased regulation of smoking; they depict smokers as amiable people despite heavy-handed efforts to restrict their habit; and, certainly in the case of the Statue of Liberty spots, they link smoking with powerful images of freedom.

Cigarette Marketing and Youth. One of the most controversial aspects of tobacco marketing involves the alleged targeting of youth populations. In 1995, concerns about such targeting led the U.S. Food and Drug Administration (FDA) to propose new rules to curtail teen smoking.

"Children are especially susceptible to the deadly temptation of tobacco and its skillful marketing," President Bill Clinton noted when he announced the restrictions.

In August 1996, President Clinton authorized FDA regulations that would:

- Require age verification to ensure cigarettes and smokeless tobacco products are sold only to customers over the age of eighteen.

- Ban vending machines and self-service displays except in certain adult locations, ban free samples, and ban sales of single cigarettes ("loosies") and packages with fewer than twenty cigarettes ("kiddie packs").

- Ban outdoor advertising within 1,000 feet of schools and playgrounds. Permit black-and-white, text-only advertising for all other outdoor advertising, including billboards, signs inside and outside of buses, and all advertising where tobacco is sold (unless the advertisement is in a place that excludes those under eighteen and is not visible from the outside).

- Permit only black-and-white, text-only advertising in publications with significant youth readership (under eighteen). Significant readership means more than 15 percent or more than 2 million. No restrictions on print advertising below these thresholds.

- Prohibit sale or giveaway of products like caps or gym bags that carry cigarette or smokeless tobacco product brand names or logos.

- Prohibit brand-name sponsorship of sporting or entertainment events, but permit sponsorship using the corporate name.

The proposed $368.5 billion settlement reached in 1997 would go even further in its restrictions against targeting minors. If enacted, it would:

- Impose financial penalties on tobacco companies if youth smoking rates do not decline substantially.

- Adopt a national licensing program for merchants selling tobacco products, with penalties for selling to minors.

- Ban all cigarette vending machines, a reliable source of tobacco for many youths.

- Elimination of all human images and cartoon characters from advertising, as well as an end to promotions through merchandise with product names or logos.

While the manufacturers of tobacco products firmly deny targeting young people in their advertising and promotional campaigns, critics find such denials less than convincing. R.J. Reynolds's 1988 introduction of Old Joe Camel, the cartoon mascot for Camel cigarettes, further fueled critics' charges that tobacco companies were pitching their products directly to kids. They argue that the use of the cartoon figure, usually in humorous situations, was a clear attempt to appeal to the interests of the very young.

Until the summer of 1997, when R.J. Reynolds announced it was sending its cartoon mascots into retirement, Joe Camel and his various camel friends remained leading spokespersons for Camel cigarettes. While R.J. Reynolds said the ads were not geared toward kids, the campaign certainly helped increase Camel sales in the youth market. In the twelve-to-nineteen age group, sales of Camel cigarettes increased from $6 million in 1988, the year Joe Camel appeared, to $476 million in 1991. In those four years, smokers under eighteen who preferred Camels rose from less than one percent to about 30 percent of the market.[19]

Commenting on a survey that studied children's recognition of popular characters such as Mickey Mouse, former U.S. Surgeon General Joycelyn Elders said: "I think that when as many of our 6-year-olds know Joe Camel as know Mickey Mouse, that says we've got a problem!"[20]

Another important aspect of the tobacco industry's marketing campaigns is to find ways to display cigarette logos and related images in locations that will be viewed by mass audiences. If nothing else, $6 billion a year certainly buys visibility. With the exception of automobiles, tobacco products are advertised more heavily than any other product in the United States. Not only do cigarette ads appear prominently in printed publications such as magazines and newspapers, but images of tobacco products are widely seen on roadside billboards, in store windows, on the sides of tall buildings and city buses, and inside many stadiums and athletic arenas.

Creative Advertising. Furthermore, despite being banned from advertising in the electronic media since

1971, the tobacco companies have found creative ways to avoid the prohibition on television advertising: being in the right place at the right time. In 1995, the U.S. Justice Department forced Philip Morris to remove many billboards from sports arenas around the country, contending that the company's Marlboro billboards were placed in strategic locations inside stadiums to guarantee visibility during television coverage of sporting events: along sidelines, above players' entrances to the arena, and behind goalposts.

While disputing that they deliberately place signs in areas to gain television exposure, the cigarette companies' products certainly do make it onto the screen in these and other ways. Their sponsorship of auto races, rodeos, tennis tournaments, and other sporting events is one of the primary routes of television exposure. During one ninety-minute car race (the Marlboro Grand Prix, by the way), the word "Marlboro" appeared on television 5,933 times, according to a study by Alan Blum, founder of the group Doctors Ought to Care.[21] Another media analysis concluded that Philip Morris picked up more than $14 million worth of television exposure through its sponsorship of "Indy" car racing in 1994. Similarly, R.J. Reynolds reaped $21 million in television time by sponsoring the Winston Cup racing series.[22]

Sponsorship of sporting events is just one part of a wider activity called "nonmedia" promotion, which plays an increasingly important role in tobacco marketing. Rather than concentrating solely on the traditional advertising layouts in magazines, cigarette companies today also devote hefty resources to things like specialty gifts and sponsorship of public entertainment.

Tobacco companies are able to promote their products through sponsorship of sporting events. During one ninety-minute car race, the word "Marlboro" appeared on television 5,933 times.

Significantly, this nonmedia advertising provides publicity for the product name, but does not carry the health-warning labels found on actual packages of cigarettes or in standard printed ads. Coupons and specialty merchandise catalogs represent other huge promotional efforts. The catalogs offer products ranging from T-shirts and baseball caps to shot glasses and lipstick holders—each with a tobacco product logo. As a measure of how important nonmedia promotions have become to cigarette manufacturers, expenditures on these items and activities have risen from 21 percent of the total advertising and promotion budget in 1975 to more than

84 percent in 1993, the latest year analyzed, according to the Federal Trade Commission.[23, 24]

In the early 1990s, a new twist on traditional marketing began to appear in the United States. Tobacco specialty stores—stores that sell only tobacco products—have made inroads into a market traditionally dominated by supermarkets by offering a very wide selection and considerably lower prices. The trend has led to some speculation that tobacco companies themselves may soon enter the retail market, rather than selling their products through outlets like supermarkets and convenience stores.

As any veteran of the advertising industry will confirm, successful marketing usually involves creating a favorable or desirable image and then associating a given product with that image. Philip Morris did this expertly with the Marlboro Man. Taken as a whole, the tobacco industry's far-reaching advertising and promotional activities also work to create images. Specifically, tobacco companies seek to reinforce the following two major perceptions:

1. Tobacco is an ordinary consumer item, no different from all the other products commonly advertised in magazines and on billboards.

2. Smoking is a very common behavior that most people enjoy and participate in.

Both of these perceptions play an important part in reinforcing the social aspects of smoking, which are discussed next.

Social Aspects

In addition to the powerful effects of tobacco marketing, factors such as social norms, group pressure, and curiosity play a part in the decision of many people—particularly young people—to begin smoking. It is interesting to note, however, that while such reasons may explain why adolescents initially try cigarettes, other factors, especially addiction, influence the decision to continue smoking.

The Appeal to Young People. Adolescence is a time of many transitions. Young people are moving from childhood to adulthood physically, socially, psychologically, and emotionally. For many young people, this is a fun-filled, happy time of life because of all the new opportunities that become available. For others, however, this time of transition is a bit rocky. Feelings of low self-esteem, low self-image, confusion, and worries about an inability to "fit in" are common at this stage of life, and these feelings make adolescents vulnerable to participate in a range of risky behaviors, including tobacco use.

For some young people, smoking serves the functions of bonding with members of their peer group, asserting their independence and maturity, and boosting their social image. Some adolescent smokers confirm that cigarette use is one way to establish their own identity.

"My parents don't smoke and a lot of my friends don't smoke," said one young cigarette smoker. "I smoke because I want to. That's it. I do it because I choose to. That's the way I am."

For all its negative connotations, smoking is an important part of the American culture. Perhaps *because* of all its negative connotations, smoking has developed a certain rebel image that many people, particularly young people, find intriguing. For generations, it has been considered an element in a rite of passage, an act that signals the beginning of adulthood and independence.

For its part, the tobacco industry stresses these types of social factors, especially peer pressure, in their explanation of why adolescents begin to use tobacco products.

"Research on youth smoking tells us that children are heavily influenced by parents, friends and family members. Peer pressure, in fact, is the single most important motivating factor outside the family," states a publication of the Tobacco Institute, a tobacco industry trade group. "Peer pressure has an enormous influence over your children, and the temptation to experiment and to be one of the group sometimes becomes too strong to resist."[25]

Critics of the tobacco companies, on the other hand, charge that cigarette marketing strategies are specifically designed to play on the unique social attitudes and the personal insecurities of adolescents. Joe Camel's "smooth character" approach and Virginia Slims' "free spirit" message are two frequently cited examples of cigarette manufacturers' attempts to directly align their products with the psychological and social needs of young people. In addition, tobacco advertisements use approaches known to appeal to youth populations.

According to a surgeon general's report:

[Cigarette] messages have become increasingly less informational, replacing words with images to portray the attractiveness and function of smoking. Cigarette advertising frequently uses human models or human-like cartoon characters to display images of youthful activities, independence, healthfulness, and adventure-seeking.[26]

Especially in the case of young people, part of the decision to smoke appears to involve some basic misunderstandings of their environment. Perhaps due to the pervasive advertising and promotion of tobacco products, many young people believe smoking is much more common than it actually is. Those who hold this view are more likely to begin smoking, according to the Centers for Disease Control and Prevention (CDC).[27]

Many young smokers also intend only to experiment with cigarettes for a while, then quit. They never suspect or desire that it could become a lifelong habit. But, according to data from the CDC, a significant number of young people never manage to quit. In one study of high school seniors, 44 percent of daily smokers believed they would no longer be smoking in five years; a follow-up study five years later revealed that 73 percent of those former students were still smoking on a daily basis.[28]

Figures such as these highlight one of the central issues in the smoking debate: the problem of addiction.

Addiction

When considering the question of why people smoke, many health professionals are convinced that the answer most often comes down to addiction. But the addiction debate remains controversial. Much of the debate hinges on two main points: whether the active ingredient in tobacco—nicotine—can be considered an addictive substance and whether cigarette manufacturers knowingly manipulate nicotine levels to create addiction in tobacco users.

For years, tobacco companies have maintained that

cigarettes are not addictive. As evidence, they contend that nicotine lacks one of the hallmarks of other addictive drugs: intoxication. Unlike cocaine or heroin or alcohol, tobacco products produce no euphoric "high." If anything, nicotine is comparable to caffeine or chocolate, according to the tobacco industry. However, most regular smokers report that cigarettes have powerful mood altering characteristics. Nicotine is capable of both stimulating and calming the user under different circumstances.

As further evidence that tobacco use is not addictive, the tobacco industry also points to the tens of millions of Americans who have kicked the smoking habit. According to 1994 statistics, more than 44 million Americans have quit smoking and roughly half of all living adults in the United States who ever smoked cigarettes have managed to quit.[29]

Instead of addiction, people continue to smoke for reasons most accurately described as personal preference, according to tobacco advocates. The perceived benefits of smoking and of nicotine, mostly relaxation and feelings of improved emotional well-being, are strong motivators, these defenders say.

Nicotine, an Addiction. In stark contrast to tobacco manufacturers, however, many leading health and medical organizations hold the position that nicotine is indeed addictive. The Office of the U.S. Surgeon General, the World Health Organization, the American Medical Association, the American Psychiatric Association, the American Psychological Association, the American Society of Addiction Medicine, and the Medical Research

Council in the United Kingdom all recognize nicotine as an addictive substance.

In an editorial response to the tobacco industry's position on addiction, the *Detroit Free Press* remarked: "Some heroin users have been known to kick their habits, too; should heroin no longer be considered addictive? To be sure, some 3,000 U.S. cigarette smokers do quit every day—roughly a third of them by dying."[30]

In his 1988 surgeon general's report, then–Surgeon General C. Everett Koop warned that "cigarettes and other forms of tobacco are addicting in the same sense as are drugs such as heroine and cocaine."[31]

Current public health leaders continue to warn consumers against the dangers of nicotine addiction. Speaking before a gathering of the National Association for the Advancement of Colored People in the mid-1990s, former FDA Commissioner Dr. David Kessler added his voice to the growing chorus of health professionals concerned about nicotine addiction.

"I strongly feel that part of my own responsibility as the Commissioner of the Food and Drug Administration is to sound the warning about the addictive nature of nicotine in tobacco. And make no mistake about it . . . nicotine is addictive."[32]

In an address to the U.S. House of Representatives Subcommittee on Health and the Environment, Kessler commented further on nicotine as an addictive substance:

> Definitions of an addictive substance may vary slightly, but they all embody some key criteria: first, compulsive use, often despite knowing the substance is harmful; second, a psychoactive effect—that is, a direct chemical effect in the brain; third, what

Former FDA Commissioner Dr. David Kessler is a staunch supporter of efforts to regulate the tobacco industry.

researchers call reinforcing behavior that conditions continued use. In addition, withdrawal symptoms occur with many drugs and occur in many cigarette smokers who try to quit. These are hallmarks of an addictive substance and nicotine meets them all.[33]

The entry of the FDA into the addiction debate is significant. This government agency has regulatory power over all drugs sold in the United States. Traditionally, nicotine has not been regulated by the FDA because it has been viewed as a natural component of tobacco products, not an ingredient intentionally used to produce effects in consumers. The regulations unveiled by President Clinton in 1996 and the negotiated settlement proposed in 1997 represent a break with this approach to nicotine.

The movement toward addiction is quite rapid, according to the 1994 surgeon general's report on the health consequences of smoking, entitled *Preventing Tobacco Use Among Young People.*

> The initiation and development of tobacco use among children and adolescents progresses in five stages: from [1] forming attitudes and beliefs about tobacco, to [2] trying, [3] experimenting with, and [4] regularly using tobacco to [5] being addicted. This process generally takes about three years.[34]

As important as the observations of doctors and scientific reports are the statements of many current and former smokers who testify to the tremendous cravings for cigarettes they experience, even long after quitting.

"When I quit smoking a few years ago, I promised myself I'd take it up again when I turned 60," said one young woman. "I can hardly wait until my 60th birthday."

In the face of such a sizable body of scientific evidence and persuasive consumer testimony, the tobacco companies' official insistence that their products are not addictive has been roundly criticized. Their public position was further damaged when, as mentioned previously, secret internal documents revealed that senior tobacco industry officials had acknowledged as long as thirty years ago that nicotine is indeed addictive.

The debate over nicotine addiction is more than an abstract argument over medical terminology. At stake is the health of millions of current and former smokers and, quite possibly, the continued existence of tobacco products and manufacturers in the United States. In addition to its important role in prompting new regulatory proposals from the FDA and its central place in the proposed settlement between tobacco companies and the state attorneys-general, huge legal battles now underway in courts throughout the United States focus on the role of addiction and the alleged efforts of tobacco companies to hide damaging information about their products. Judgments in favor of millions of "nicotine-dependent" smokers and their families could well bankrupt even the wealthy tobacco companies.

The issues that fuel the current tobacco battles, some of which are discussed in more detail later in this book, will likely remain in dispute for a very long time. Once they are settled new issues will inevitably arise to replace them. The story of tobacco in our society is a long and colorful one and future chapters wait to be written.

Today, as in every other day of the year, more than 3,000 adolescents in the United States will smoke their first cigarette on their way to becoming regular smokers as adults. During their lifetime we can expect that, of these 3,000 young people, approximately 20 will be murdered, 30 will die in traffic accidents, and nearly 750 will be killed by a smoking-related disease.[1]

—National Cancer Institute

3

The Costs of Smoking

Introducing legislation in March 1995 designed to discourage smoking by increasing federal cigarette taxes, Democratic Senator Bill Bradley of New Jersey put the devastating health effects of tobacco use into perspective. Smoking, he pointed out, kills more Americans every year than alcohol, heroin, crack, automobile and airplane accidents, homicides, suicides, and AIDS combined.

The senator's observation helps to illustrate the dimensions of the quiet epidemic of tobacco-related deaths that grips the United States. For all the media attention given to the serious problems of illegal drug use, a legal drug kills more people in the United States. For all the attention generated by fiery airplane crashes, a much smaller burning ember claims many more victims. For all the attention given to a relatively new and mysterious health crisis such as AIDS, a much more familiar and better-understood epidemic continues to kill far more people every year.

With more than four hundred thousand American deaths attributed to cigarette smoking annually, the costs of this epidemic are truly staggering, in economic, human, and social terms. In 1993, the University of California and the federal Centers for Disease Control and Prevention (CDC) attempted to put some price tags on the medical costs associated with cigarette smoking. In total, they estimated that smoking led to medical expenses of about $50 billion in 1993, including $26.9 billion for hospital expenditures, $15.5 billion for physician expenditures, $4.9 billion for nursing home expenditures, $1.8 billion for prescription drugs, and $900 million for home health care.

Furthermore, these estimates of the medical costs stemming from smoking were considered by the authors to be low because they did not take into account things such as the cost of burn care resulting from cigarette-related fires, care for low-birth-weight infants of mothers who smoke, or care for people suffering diseases stemming from exposure to environmental tobacco smoke (secondhand smoke). If these additional figures were calculated, it is likely the total economic burden of cigarette smoking would exceed $100 billion per year.[2]

In addition to the many smoking-related medical conditions that researchers can track and assign a dollar figure to, there are a host of other costs associated with tobacco use that are not so easily measured. These are the human costs of tobacco use and they should not be overlooked. For example, children who smoke cigarettes are much more likely to become heroin, cocaine, and crack

Cigarettes are a factor in many automobile accidents. Five people were injured in this collision, which occurred when the driver lost control while trying to retrieve a burning cigarette from the car's rear seat.

addicts than children who never use cigarettes, according to the Center on Addiction and Substance Abuse at Columbia University.[3] The role of tobacco as a so-called "gateway" drug—a substance that encourages or leads to the use of other drugs—is an important factor to consider in this regard.

This chapter examines some of the most prominent health hazards of smoking, then looks beyond the health concerns to consider some of the other effects of smoking on society. These other effects include the social issues surrounding current attempts to restrict smoking in public areas, the difficult question of who should pay for smokers' health problems, and instances of alleged discrimination against smokers.

The Health Costs of Smoking

Cancer. Of the more than five hundred thousand Americans who die from cancer each year, about one third develop the disease as a result of their use of cigarettes and other tobacco products.[4] Smokers lose an average of fifteen years of their lives. The risk of dying of lung cancer is twenty-two times higher for men who smoke and twelve times higher for women who smoke than for nonsmokers.[5]

Lung cancer is the single largest category of cancer deaths in the United States (an estimated 146,000 deaths in 1992) and smoking is responsible for 90 percent of all lung cancers.[6] According to the National Cancer Institute, the risk of developing lung cancer and other smoking-associated cancers is related to total lifetime exposure to cigarette smoke. Total lifetime exposure is

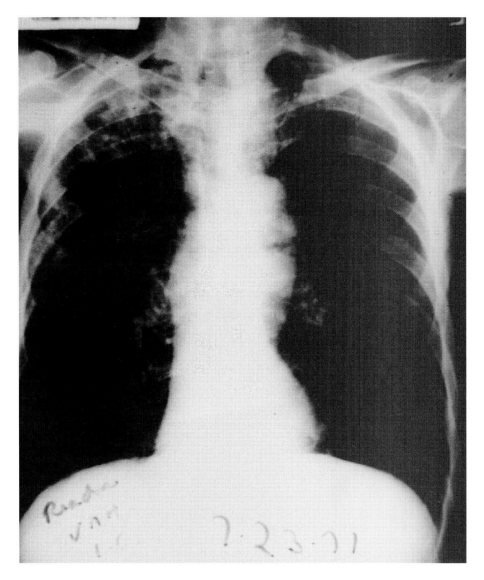

Doctors use chest x-rays to diagnose lung cancer. Lung cancer is the single largest category of cancer deaths in the United States, and smoking is responsible for 90 percent of these deaths.

measured by the number of cigarettes smoked each day, the age at which smoking began, and the number of years a person has smoked.

In addition to lung cancer, smoking also substantially increases the risk of developing cancers of the mouth, larynx, pharynx, esophagus, bladder, kidney, cervix, and pancreas. Cigarette smoking is also believed to cause about 14 percent of all leukemias, and 30 percent of all cancer deaths.

There also appear to be associations between smoking and breast cancer. In a study that focused on smokers with breast cancer, the American Cancer Society reported in 1994 that a woman's risk of dying from breast cancer increases by 25 percent if she is a smoker. Several possible explanations were offered.

"For example, smokers may have impaired immune systems, they may not obtain routine mammographic screenings, or smoking may cause a direct deleterious [harmful] effect on survival,"[7] said Dr. Eugenia Calle of the American Cancer Society, who authored the report.

To a great extent, smoking has covered up some major victories won in the decades-long battle against cancer. In 1995, one of the leaders of the anticancer campaign, Dr. Vincent Devita, Jr., singled out cigarette smoking in his remarks about the nation's struggle to defeat cancer:

> The incidence of lung cancer has risen so much over the last 30 to 40 years that many advances have been obscured behind a cloud of cigarette smoke. However, we are now seeing in groups—such as white males, where smoking prevalence began to decline in the late 1960s—a decline in the incidence and mortality

[death rate] of lung cancer. If you remove the cancer mortality resulting from smoking, you'd see substantial declines in cancer mortality all the way up to age 85. So obviously, the more effective anti-smoking campaigns become the more visible will be the progress against cancer.[8]

Cardiovascular Disease. Cardiovascular disease (CVD) is the number one cause of death in the United States. Smoking substantially increases the risk of CVD. Coronary heart disease, stroke, and peripheral vascular disease are some of the health outcomes firmly associated with smoking. Cigarettes caused nearly one hundred eighty thousand deaths from CVD in the United States in 1990.

The American Heart Association reports that a possible explanation for the increase in CVD is that smoking accelerates the process of atherosclerosis (hardening of the arteries) by damaging blood vessels. In atherosclerosis, deposits of fat, cholesterol, and other substances clog the interior walls of arteries. As the arteries become lined with layers of deposits they are narrowed and the flow of blood is reduced. By adding the equivalent of ten years of aging to their arteries, smokers increase their risk of heart attack and stroke, according to Dr. Grethe Tell, professor and head of epidemiology at Bowman Gray School of Medicine in Winston-Salem, North Carolina.[9]

Reproductive Health Problems. About 25 percent of pregnant women in the United States are believed to smoke. Smoking during pregnancy is associated with certain birth defects, premature birth, low birth weight, and high rates of sudden infant death syndrome (SIDS). An array of negative health effects follow children born to

49

women who smoked during pregnancy, including behavioral problems and learning difficulties.[10]

Recent medical studies also link smoking with risks of miscarriage and other infant health problems. A 1995 report in the *Journal of Family Practice* concluded that maternal smoking causes about 115,000 miscarriages and the deaths of about 5,600 infants in the United States every year. The study concluded that the number of pre-natal and infant deaths due to smoking outnumbered those caused by homicide and child abuse.[11]

Nicotine, like other drugs, can also have important effects on an individual's nutritional state. In a study of 400 pregnant women, researchers discovered that smok-ers had 15 percent less vitamin C in their bloodstreams than nonsmokers, despite higher intakes of the vitamin. Newborn babies of smokers also had lower than normal levels of vitamin C.

Lung Diseases. Lung diseases are among the leading causes of death and disability in the United States, and cigarette smoking has long been recognized as a principal contributing factor. More than 25 million persons have chronic bronchitis, emphysema, asthma, or other lung diseases. These diseases, excluding cancer, account for 222,000 deaths annually and are a contributing cause to perhaps an equal number of additional deaths.[12]

The typical pattern of many lung diseases, including those caused by smoking, involves a long period of time—perhaps twenty, thirty, or forty years—during which no symptoms are evident. However, over these years, there is accumulating lung damage. Patients' final years of suffering from lung diseases are usually marked by severe physical restrictions and great pain.

If a woman smokes during pregnancy, it can lead to many health problems in her infant.

Environmental Tobacco Smoke—Secondhand Smoke.
The topic of environmental tobacco smoke (ETS), a
mixture of the smoke given off by the burning end of
cigarettes, pipes, or cigars, and the smoke exhaled by
smokers, has gained widespread public attention in recent
years. Much of the attention was prompted by a report
released in 1993 by the Environmental Protection
Agency (EPA), which concluded that widespread
exposure to ETS "presents a serious and substantial
public health risk."

According to the National Cancer Institute, when a
cigarette is smoked, about half of the smoke generated is
sidestream smoke emitted from the burning cigarette
between puffs. This sidestream smoke contains essentially
all of the same carcinogenic (cancer-causing) and toxic
agents that have been identified in the mainstream smoke
inhaled by the smoker, but at greater levels.

The mixture of smoke known as ETS, or secondhand
smoke, contains more than four thousand substances.
About sixty of these substances have been positively identified as either carcinogens (cancer-causing substances) or
other compounds that initiate or promote tumor growth.
These compounds include tar, carbon monoxide, hydro-
gen cyanide, phenols, ammonia, formaldehyde, benzene,
nitrosamine, and nicotine.

In a move that stirred considerable controversy, the
1993 EPA report classified secondhand smoke as a so-
called Group A carcinogen. In other words, ETS is listed
among a class of substances known to cause cancer in
humans. Other Group A carcinogens include asbestos,
benzene, and radon. Only ETS has actually been shown
to cause cancer at typical environmental levels.

52

When a cigarette is smoked, about half of the smoke generated is sidestream smoke, which contains all of the same cancer-causing agents as the mainstream smoke inhaled by the smoker. Secondhand smoke causes three thousand lung cancer deaths per year in the United States.

In particular, the EPA report stated that secondhand smoke is responsible for approximately three thousand lung cancer deaths and twelve thousand non-lung cancer deaths per year among nonsmokers in the United States. This finding raised significant alarm because of the great many places—including homes and workplaces—populated by both smokers and nonsmokers at the same time. With ETS linked to cancer, secondhand smoke immediately became recognized as not only an annoyance to many nonsmokers, but a genuine health hazard as well.

In addition to cancer, studies also link ETS with other respiratory conditions, such as coughing, phlegm production, chest discomfort, and reduced lung function. Respiratory health problems from ETS are especially common in children and infants. The National Cancer Institute issued the following summary of more than fifty medical studies that detail the connections between ETS and various respiratory ailments:

- ETS exposure due to parental smoking, especially the mother's, contributes to 150,000 to 300,000 cases annually of lower respiratory tract infection (pneumonia, bronchitis, and other infections) in infants and children under 18 months of age; 7,500 to 15,000 of these cases will require hospitalization.

- ETS exposure is associated with increased respiratory irritation (cough, phlegm production, and wheezing) and middle ear infections, as well as upper respiratory tract symptoms (sore throats and colds) in infants and children.

- ETS exposure increases the number of episodes and the severity of asthma in children who already have the disease. The EPA report estimates that ETS worsens the condition in 200,000 to 1 million asthmatic children. Moreover, ETS exposure increases the number of new cases of asthma in children who have not previously exhibited symptoms.

- ETS exposure within the uterus and in infancy can alter lung function and structure and create other changes that are known to predispose children to long-term pulmonary risks.

- In the United States, sudden infant death syndrome (SIDS) is the major cause of death in infants between the ages of one month and one year, and the linkage with maternal smoking is well established. Current evidence strongly suggests that infants whose mothers smoke are at an increased risk of dying of SIDS.[13]

In addition to these respiratory ailments, there is also evidence that ETS is a risk factor for cardiovascular disease.[14] In fact, according to researchers at the University of California-San Francisco (UCSF), nonsmokers' cardiovascular systems are the most vulnerable to damage by environmental tobacco smoke. The health effects of ETS on nonsmokers must be considered differently from its effects on smokers, they contend.

"People who smoke cigarettes are chronically and continually adversely affecting the cardiovascular system, which adapts to compensate for all the deleterious [harmful] effects of smoking," wrote Stanton Glantz and William Parmley of UCSF in the *Journal of the American*

Medical Association. "Nonsmokers, however, do not have the 'benefit' of this adaptation, so the effects of passive smoking on nonsmokers are much greater than on smokers."[15]

These and other reports on secondhand smoke, many of which were met with great fanfare in the media and considerable alarm in much of the general public, prompted irritation and outrage in other circles. Because it formed the basis for many smoking restrictions throughout the country, the EPA report, in particular, seized the attention of the tobacco companies and some members of Congress friendly to tobacco interests. To put it mildly, these disgruntled groups were not impressed with the agency's findings or its methods of scientific investigation.

The tobacco companies were so unhappy with the EPA report that they filed a lawsuit seeking its withdrawal by the agency. The tobacco companies contend that the EPA improperly selected which health studies to review, lowered its standards in assessing the health risks of ETS, and used a controversial technique of combining the results of different research studies.

"The EPA cherry-picked what it wants the American people to know," said Daniel W. Donahue, senior vice president–litigation and deputy general counsel for R.J. Reynolds Tobacco Company, asserting that the tobacco industry has been directly and negatively impacted by the agency's report. "Without those strategies, we believe the EPA quite simply could not reach what is in essence an unsupportable conclusion—that ETS is a Class A human carcinogen."[16]

The EPA report also irritated some leading members of

Congress, including Representative Thomas J. Bliley, Jr., of Virginia (Republican), a staunch supporter of the tobacco industry and the top congressional recipient of tobacco political action committee contributions since 1985. Accusing the EPA of trying to "scare the public," Bliley called the ETS analysis an "abuse of science and the scientific process to further a political agenda."

"EPA's willingness to distort science in order to justify its classification of ETS as a 'Group A' or 'known human' carcinogen seems to stem from the Agency's determination early on to advocate smoking bans and restrictions as a socially desirable goal," he said.

Bliley expressed additional concern about the use of the report's conclusions to excuse the mistreatment of smokers. This concern prompted him to observe that "if claims made in the report are invalid, as appears to be the case, the likely consequence will be additional unjustified harassment of and discrimination against smokers . . ."[17]

In response to the strong criticisms of its secondhand smoke report, the EPA issued a statement in June 1994 reiterating that it "absolutely stands by its scientific and well documented report." Furthermore, the agency defended the report's main conclusions and attempted to address some of the more inflammatory charges levied by opponents.

> The evidence is clear and consistent: secondhand smoke is a cause of lung cancer in adults who don't smoke. EPA has never claimed that minimal exposure to secondhand smoke poses [a] huge individual cancer risk. Even though the lung cancer risk from secondhand smoke is relatively small compared to the risk from direct smoking, unlike a smoker who

chooses to smoke, the nonsmoker's risk is often involuntary. In addition, exposure to secondhand smoke varies tremendously among exposed individuals. For those who must live or work in close proximity to one or more smokers, the risk would certainly be greater than for those less exposed.[18]

Finally, the EPA dismissed suggestions that it was part of a larger effort to ban smoking, stating, "The claim that the government is attempting to bring back prohibition—this time for cigarettes—is a complete fabrication and utter nonsense. EPA's interest is to provide information to protect the nonsmoker from involuntary exposure to a hazardous substance."

At the present time, the legal battle over the EPA report is still being waged in federal court. Meanwhile, the larger controversy concerning the harmfulness of secondhand smoke continues to be debated in homes, office buildings, factories, restaurants, and virtually every other place where smokers and nonsmokers gather together.

The Social Costs of Smoking

As indicated in some of the statements regarding secondhand smoke, the movement against tobacco in recent years has escalated considerably. While environmental tobacco smoke might once have been regarded as a trivial matter, the most undesirable characteristic of which was its tendency to make one's clothes and hair smell bad, that is certainly no longer the case. Today, there are genuine health concerns to be weighed and nonsmokers are demanding protection. The disputes that commonly arise over the issue can create serious rifts between smokers and nonsmokers, even when the parties involved are friends and family members.

The debate over smoking has other tangible social effects as well, most notably in the form of bans and restrictions. Efforts to control the sale, promotion, and use of tobacco products are common in most parts of the country today. In addition, there is rising debate over the question of who should pay for the tremendous cost of providing health care to smokers after they develop the diseases that usually follow from their habit. Last, but not least, there is also the question of the dwindling social acceptance of smokers. As the habit becomes less socially acceptable, some people are concerned about the potential for discrimination against smokers.

Tobacco Control Efforts. President Bill Clinton's actions in 1996 to restrict tobacco advertising and youth access to tobacco products and the proposed settlement between tobacco companies and state attorneys-general in 1997 gained widespread public attention, but other attempts to control tobacco have been taking root at the state and local levels. As of 1994, forty-six states and the District of Columbia had implemented some type of smoking restriction, ranging from the prohibition of smoking on school buses to comprehensive clean indoor air laws banning smoking in nearly all public places. In addition, many municipalities have passed ordinances restricting smoking.

Some of these bans at the state and local level have gained national attention. For instance, after months of public debate and intense lobbying by the tobacco industry, New York City adopted a law in 1995 that severely restricts smoking in public places. The Smoke-Free Air Act, which outlaws smoking in restaurants that seat more than thirty-five people, outdoor arenas, parks, and most businesses and workplaces, was strongly criticized by the restaurant, hospitality, and tourism industries. In addition, the Philip Morris Company, which has its world headquarters in New York City, threatened to leave its Park Avenue offices and end its financial support of New York arts organizations if the restrictions were adopted.

A sampling of some other smoking bans and restrictions from across the United States includes:

- **California:** The California Smokefree Workplace Act prohibits smoking in nearly all of California's enclosed places of employment. The measure prohibits smoking in offices and restaurants, but excludes certain locations such as gaming clubs, bars, tobacco shops, and 65 percent of hotel and motel rooms. "California is on its way to becoming the first smoke-free state in the union," said Paul Knepprath, spokesperson for the American Lung Association of California.

- **Texas:** The Texas Board of Criminal Justice outlawed the use and possession of all tobacco products in state prisons. The ban applies to all inmates and prison employees on state property.

- **Maryland:** One of the nation's strictest statewide smoking bans went into effect in 1995. The law covers nearly every workplace, including factories, stores, colleges, prisons, and even certain company-owned automobiles. Exemptions are allowed for restaurants, bars, taverns, private clubs, and hotel and motel rooms. The Maryland measure has special significance because it is the first tobacco-producing state to enact a law to restrict workers' exposure to secondhand smoke.

• **Baltimore, Maryland:** The City of Baltimore restricts outdoor cigarette advertising within city limits. These restrictions are focused on "advertisements that most directly affect minors where they live, attend school, attend church and engage in recreation activities." Certain designated business and industrial zones are exempted.

• **Las Cruces, New Mexico:** The City Council voted in March 1995 to adopt a wide-ranging ban on smoking. Affected locations include restaurants, elevators, public transportation, shopping malls, stores, sports arenas, public rest rooms, museums, art galleries, and banks.

Nationally, too, there have been some serious efforts to restrict smoking in certain areas. A federal law that went into effect in 1994 restricts smoking in nearly all public places where federal assistance is provided for day-care and other services to children.

The Occupational Safety and Health Administration (OSHA), the federal government agency charged with protecting the health and safety of American workers, released a proposal in 1994 to require employers throughout the United States to ban workplace smoking or to provide designated smoking areas that are vented to the outside of the building.

Across the nation, various fast-food restaurants have begun to implement smoking restrictions in recent years. Dunkin' Donuts, for example, instituted a mandatory

Smoking is prohibited in most office buildings and many other public places.

smoke-free policy in its three thousand outlets throughout the United States in 1995. McDonalds Corporation also banned smoking at its company-owned restaurants and actively encourages its franchises to follow suit.

Other tobacco control efforts involve not bans or restrictions, but taxes on tobacco products. The tax proposal offered by Senator Bradley, mentioned at the beginning of this chapter, is one example. Often, the taxes are combined with legislative mandates to fund and operate tobacco prevention and research programs. Laws in Arizona and California, for instance, require that a portion of the money raised by state tobacco taxes be used for research into tobacco-related diseases and school and community prevention programs.

In California, a coalition of nonprofit health groups, including the American Cancer Society and the American Lung Association, claim that in the five years since California's antismoking program was initiated, it has reduced smoking by 28 percent, a rate two to three times faster than the national average. This translates into one million fewer smokers.

The California program was born of the 1988 decision by voters to adopt Proposition 99, which hiked the state tobacco tax by 25 cents per pack and specified how the new funds should be spent. Five percent of the revenue was set aside for tobacco-related research and 20 percent was earmarked for tobacco education programs. Some of the funds have also been used to produce antitobacco advertising in California. Throughout its brief history, the program has been subjected to repeated legislative and executive attempts to divert its funding, but so far it has survived and has won praise as "the country's best disease prevention program."

Also, since 1989, the program has saved the California economy an estimated $1 billion per year, including $211 million a year in direct state health care costs, according to an evaluation by the University of California-San Diego.

Another tobacco control strategy involves the use of advertising to counter the positive images of smoking portrayed by cigarette manufacturers. In 1995, the Massachusetts Department of Public Health developed some particularly compelling antismoking ads, one of which featured a former cigarette company model, who now has throat cancer, encouraging people to avoid smoking.

In general, measures to restrict smoking have met with approval from nonsmokers and fury from the tobacco industry and many smokers. The OSHA proposal to virtually ban smoking in the workplace, for example, resulted in more mail and comments than any other proposal in the agency's twenty-five-year history. The vast majority of the comments condemned the attempt to regulate workplace smoking.

The National Smokers Alliance, a national coalition that fights what it considers excessive regulation and taxation aimed at smokers, has been particularly vocal in its objections to many tobacco control initiatives. The group's president, Thomas Humber, called the Maryland statewide smoking ban "one more example of regulation that will destroy business, one more freedom lost, and one more sign that some politicians simply do not get it."[19]

Humber also criticized antismoking organizations for seeking additional tobacco controls.

"As anticipated, anti-smoking extremists will never be satisfied with a 'mere' ban on smoking in public places," he said. "Their real goal has been, and always will be, total prohibition of tobacco in the United States."[20]

Who Should Pay? As noted earlier in this chapter, smoking is a habit that carries a tremendously high financial cost to society. In recent years, as smoking has become less socially acceptable, there have been occasional moves to try to recoup some of the billions of dollars spent annually to care for ill smokers.

Recent proposals have come in two basic forms: increasing taxes on cigarettes and forcing tobacco companies to reimburse states for the cost of providing medical treatment to smokers who develop smoking-related ailments.

The proposal to raise cigarette taxes gained special attention in 1994, during the debate over national health care reform. Higher cigarette taxes, some argued, would not only help finance the cost of providing health insurance to the 38 million uninsured Americans, but they would also likely discourage smoking, especially among adolescents.

The current federal tax on a pack of cigarettes is twenty-four cents. State and local authorities also may apply taxes. On average, the total tax is fifty-six cents per pack in the United States, one of the lowest cigarette tax rates in any developed nation.

One suggestion to increase the federal excise tax on cigarettes called for the creation of a Smoker's Accountability Trust to help pay for antismoking programs,

Cigarette smoking carries a tremendous financial cost to society. There is much debate over who should bear this cost.

research, and medical expenses. Any such move to hike tobacco taxes would have to overcome both a strong pro-tobacco lobby in Washington, D.C., and the strong antitax sentiments of most Americans.

Several states have developed a novel approach to recoup the cost of treating Medicaid patients with smoking-related diseases. Florida, Minnesota, Mississippi, and West Virginia became the first four of fifteen states to press lawsuits against the tobacco industry arguing that the tobacco companies are liable for selling a product that results in sickness and death. Since many smokers seek medical treatment under the coverage of Medicaid, a state-run health insurance plan, the lawsuits contend that the tobacco companies should be held financially accountable. The state of Florida, for instance, is seeking $1.43 billion. These cases are still making their way through the courts although they could be settled as part of the proposed agreement reached in the summer of 1997.

Regardless of the outcomes in these cases, such legal steps appear to signal a new push in society to see the tobacco companies take greater financial responsibility for the health consequences of their products.

Discrimination Against Smokers? As the trend away from treating smoking as a socially acceptable activity has accelerated, some smokers have complained that they now suffer unfair treatment. Such complaints arise most frequently in employment situations.

According to one nationwide survey of employers, more than 55 percent of companies in the United States completely prohibit smoking while employees are on their property. Only about 5 percent allow smoking in all

A Special Message for Smokers from the U.S. Environmental Protection Agency

This is a difficult time to be a smoker. As the public becomes more aware that smoking is not only a hazard to you but also to others, nonsmokers are becoming more outspoken, and smokers are finding themselves a beleaguered group.

If you choose to smoke, here are some things you can do to help protect the people close to you:

- Don't smoke around children. Their lungs are very susceptible to smoke. If you are expecting a child, quit smoking.

- Take an active role in the development of your company's smoking policy. Encourage the offering of smoking cessation programs for those who want them.

- Keep your home smoke free. Nonsmokers can get lung cancer from exposure to your smoke. Because smoke lingers in the air, people may be exposed even if they are not present while you smoke. If you must smoke inside, limit smoking to a room where you can open windows for cross-ventilation. Be sure the room in which you smoke has a working smoke detector to lessen the risk of fire.

- Test your home for radon. Radon contamination in combination with smoking is a much greater health risk than either one individually.

- Don't smoke in an automobile with the windows closed if passengers are present. The high concentration of smoke in a small, closed compartment substantially increases the exposure of other passengers.

More than 2 million people quit smoking every year, most of them on their own, without the aid of a program or medication. If you want to quit smoking, assistance is available.

areas. Some smokers, however, feel no-smoking policies have gone too far.

Not only are most smokers required to leave the building in which they work if they wish to have a cigarette, but some companies refuse to hire people who smoke. The employer's justification for not hiring smokers often involves an interest in protecting the health and well-being of current employees. In addition, the decision may be motivated by the knowledge that smokers are a greater statistical risk than nonsmokers. Smokers are more frequently involved in workplace accidents and they use the company's health care benefits more than their nonsmoking counterparts. These characteristics make smokers more expensive to employ, according to many business managers.

Regardless of the reasons that motivate companies to push smokers outdoors or to decide against hiring them, the policies leave many smokers feeling like the victims of discrimination. Worse, they realize their habit has become so despised that they are unlikely to receive much public sympathy for their troubles. Some of the anti-smoking policies that have resulted in dismissals are being challenged in court, but the movement against smoking—in the workplace and elsewhere—has continued to gather momentum.

As one writer put it, "Smoking is seen, and smelled, as an insult to civilization. It is also one of the few insults that civilization can forcefully address."[21]

One important thing that every teenager in this country needs to know before deciding to smoke his or her first cigarette is how one cigarette industry official viewed the business of selling cigarettes: "We are, then, in the business of selling nicotine, an addictive drug . . ."[1]

—Dr. David A. Kessler,
former commissioner of the Food and Drug Administration

4

At-Risk Populations

Smoking is truly an equal opportunity killer. People of all races and ages die as a result of smoking. Both male and female smokers suffer the same fate. Wealthy people smoking in mansions develop lung cancer that kills them just as dead as someone smoking in public housing.

There are, however, certain segments of the population that one might identify as "at-risk" groups. These are groups that can be singled out for some special attention because of circumstances that predispose them to picking up the smoking habit. Four such groups are: youth, women, minorities, and people living in poverty.

The U.S. Surgeon General estimates that 3 million teenagers and an additional one hundred thousand children under age thirteen smoke.[2] Dr. David Kessler, the former commissioner of the FDA has referred to smoking as a "pediatric disease."[3] The point here is that tobacco use is a major element in a great many young

71

people's lives and that it can and does have lifelong consequences.

Women and girls are another group with special smoking-related concerns. Even before lung cancer surpassed breast cancer as the leading cause of cancer death in women, smoking was being labeled a feminist issue. In addition to the cancer trends, female smokers face a string of unique health concerns, including reproductive problems and increased risk of heart disease.

Tobacco has also left a legacy of disease and death in many minority groups and among persons living in poverty. While young African Americans are showing some recent encouraging signs in rejecting the use of tobacco, the damaging health effects of tobacco continue to take a high toll among certain ethnic groups.

Young People

While statistics can never tell the whole story, the figures on adolescent tobacco use are noteworthy:

- Approximately 3 million U.S. adolescents are smokers.

- About three thousand teenagers start smoking every day.

- Overall, about one third of high-school-aged adolescents in the United States smoke or use smokeless tobacco.

- Between one third and one half of the young people who try cigarettes become daily smokers.

- Adolescents smoke about 1 billion packs of cigarettes each year.

- The average age at which smokers try their first cigarette is fourteen and a half years.

- Between 80 and 90 percent of smokers begin smoking before the age of eighteen.

- Most young people who smoke regularly are addicted to nicotine and experience the same symptoms as adults.

Adolescence is a critical period of life for many different reasons. A lot of decisions are made during this time that tend to have a lasting effect on the direction of an individual's life. This is not to suggest that every choice made in the junior year of high school is entered into a permanent record book that will be one's constant companion throughout life. But many of the habits and attitudes developed at this stage of life do tend to be carried forward into adulthood. With regard to smoking in particular, adolescence is a crucial time. If someone is going to smoke, this is usually the period in which they will begin.

There are many factors that enter into a teenager's decision to smoke. Since adolescence is a time of exploration, smoking is seen by some as experimental—something to try for a while. Other adolescents view smoking as an activity they can participate in with a group of friends, a form of bonding with peers. Some young people see smoking as a way to improve their social image.

Looking at this environment, in which young people are trying out new things and looking for opportunities to take the next steps in their lives, it is also necessary to consider the actions of tobacco manufacturers and their agenda, which is to attract new buyers for their products.

Attracting New Users. Advertising that promotes smoking as a symbol of freedom and defiance has been used to great effect in youth populations. These advertisements convey powerful messages about being independent and mature, about being popular and seeking adventure. Some adolescents, particularly those with low self-esteem and low self-image, may be inclined to perceive smoking as a behavior that could enhance their image. While tobacco promotion alone cannot be said to "cause" adolescent smoking, it is an important part of the mix, a factor that "fosters the uptake of smoking," as the U.S. Surgeon General stated in 1994.[4]

Many people are particularly concerned about a shift in the tobacco manufacturers' marketing strategies, which appear to make young people special targets. Promotional merchandise, featuring tobacco companies' brand names and logos on baseball caps and T-shirts, as well as designer clothing, earrings, and leather jackets, appeals especially to younger audiences. The regulations announced by President Clinton in 1996 and the proposed settlement between the tobacco companies and the state attorneys-general aim to close the door on this particular marketing strategy.

Tobacco companies also go to great lengths to seek out the young crowd. Philip Morris traveled to South Padre Island, Texas, a popular spring break destination, to promote its Marlboro brand. The company reportedly handed out ten thousand free cigarette lighters and five thousand free T-shirts to young spring breakers in 1995.

In addition to cigarettes, many young Americans also have become regular users of smokeless tobacco—chewing tobacco and snuff. About 20 percent of high-school-aged boys chew tobacco or dip snuff, according to recent estimates from the Centers for Disease Control and Prevention (CDC). Like cigarette smokers, users of smokeless tobacco products are likely to become addicted to nicotine. In fact, recent reports indicate that manufacturers of smokeless tobacco may employ a "graduation theory," whereby young users are first introduced to low-nicotine starter products that are milder tasting and more flavored. As nicotine dependence grows, users are said to "graduate" to other brands with higher nicotine levels.

Such developments come despite tobacco company programs that are supposedly designed to curtail youth access to tobacco products. For example, Philip Morris runs a program called "It's the Law," which distributes information to retailers explaining that it is illegal to sell cigarettes to minors. UST, the top smokeless tobacco company, has taken the step of labeling all its advertising and promotional items with a warning that states, "Not for sale to minors."

State laws prohibit stores from selling cigarettes and other tobacco products to anyone under the age of eighteen. However, a 1995 report from the Department of Health and Human Services showed that most states do not enforce these "youth access" laws. As a result, it is estimated that at least half of all cigarettes smoked by minors every year are acquired illegally.[5]

Undoubtedly, advertising and promotional efforts reach young people. The effect of this appears to be considerable. In a survey conducted by the CDC in 1993, 86 percent of smokers aged twelve to eighteen reported that they most frequently purchased these three brands: Marlboro, Camel, and Newport. These same three brands were also the most heavily advertised in 1993. Adolescents' preference for Camel cigarettes did not parallel overall market preferences, but did follow a large increase in Camel advertising expenditures. Since the Joe Camel advertising campaign began, Camel's market share among teens climbed from 0.5 percent to 32.8 percent. The figure for smoking adults who choose Camels remains mostly unchanged.

Women

The CDC estimates that 22 million women, about 22.5 percent of all women in the United States, are smokers.[6] About three quarters of these female smokers report that they are dependent on cigarettes.[7]

Tragically, the statistics also show that today's female smokers are pursuing the worst of all possible options: they are starting earlier and they are smoking more. According to the U.S. Surgeon General, the health problems associated with smoking are determined by the duration and amount of tobacco use. Starting young and smoking a lot is the worst combination.

If this trend continues, the consequences of these choices will show up in the future in terms of increased cancers, heart disease, reproductive problems, osteoporosis (brittle bones), and the other serious ailments associated with cigarette smoking. Studies also indicate that women who smoke and take oral contraceptives face a greater risk of dying of cardiovascular disease than women who neither smoke nor use the pill.

The results of an earlier increase in smoking by women are only recently beginning to be seen in medical statistics. Breast cancer, long the leading cause of cancer death in women, was surpassed in 1987 by lung cancer. More than fifty-five thousand women a year now die of lung cancer, which accounts for about 22 percent of all female cancer deaths.[8] The rise in lung cancer, once a rare disease in women, can be traced to the rise of female smoking during the late 1960s and early 1970s.

More specifically, some researchers track the dramatic rise in lung cancer death rates to the introduction in 1967 of several so-called women's brands of cigarettes. Prior to that time, there was a slowly increasing rate of smoking initiation by adolescent girls. In 1967, however, the tobacco industry introduced brands such as Virginia Slims, Silva Thins, and Eve cigarettes, which were marketed heavily to women. Corresponding to this new marketing approach, the rate at which adolescent girls took up smoking jumped notably.

Women have long been the target of special attention from tobacco companies, as mentioned earlier in this book. Through a heavy concentration of cigarette advertisements in women's magazines and sponsorship of women's athletic and fashion events, the tobacco industry's message is delivered with relative ease to an important segment of the market. The gist of the tobacco advertising efforts aimed at women associate smoking with sexual attractiveness, physical fitness, and female independence.

"[Major] themes of female adolescence—body image,

popularity, success, fashion—are emphasized powerfully in cigarette advertising designed for women," observed Dr. Ellen Gritz in an editorial in a leading medical journal. "The focus on thinness with the implication that smoking serves as a means of weight control has had a strong influence on young women."[9]

During early adolescence, girls appear to be particularly susceptible to tobacco advertising, as well as other messages concerning image. Overall, girls' assessment of their physical appearance and self-worth is much lower than boys during this time of life. Faced with uncertainty about appropriate gender roles and the social expectations concerning body weight and shape, girls have proven to be vulnerable to both the product and the image being sold by cigarette manufacturers.

Researchers note that women have traditionally enjoyed greater longevity than men, but they also note that such a pattern is not inevitable. Smoking is perhaps the one activity most likely to erode that history of longer life.

Minorities and the Poor

Sometimes it seems there is only bad news to report in this area. In the case of smoking rates among African-American young people, though, there is surprisingly good news to relate.

A federal survey found that only 4.4 percent of African-American high school seniors were smoking in 1993. In comparison, 22.9 percent of white high school seniors were smokers. The 1993 statistics represent a huge decline from 1976, when 26.8 percent of African-American students had smoked.

Many adolescent girls smoke cigarettes to control their weight. They desperately try to meet the stereotypical body image portrayed on television and in fashion magazines.

The reasons for the dramatic downward trend are many. Cultural factors, such as vocal opposition to smoking and cigarette advertising by prominent African-American leaders, have helped. Along with others, the Reverend Jesse Brown in Philadelphia and the Reverend Calvin O. Butts in New York City have led successful campaigns against tobacco company plans to market so-called African-American brands.

Family influences and changing attitudes among young African Americans themselves about what sorts of activities are enjoyable also contributed to the decline. There is also some evidence that while young white women appear to use smoking for weight control, young African-American women do not view tobacco in this way.

The encouraging findings appear at a time when events convince many in the African-American community that they are the target of tobacco company pitches. The brief appearance in 1994 and 1995 of a brand called "X" cigarettes, packaged in black, green, and red colors, outraged many African-American leaders, who accused the manufacturer of trying to capitalize on the memory of Malcolm X. "X" cigarettes were withdrawn from the market shortly thereafter.

In contrast, African-American adults have somewhat higher rates of smoking than their white counterparts and much higher rates of smoking-related diseases, such as lung cancer. This may be due to the fact that, overall, African Americans smoke more and for longer periods of time than whites. In general, African Americans also tend to smoke cigarettes with higher tar and nicotine levels.

Other minority groups in the United States are not

faring as well as young African Americans in the battle
against tobacco use. In a 1992 review of cigarette
smoking among adults in the United States, the smoking
rate was highest in the Native American and Alaskan
Native groups.[10] Smokeless tobacco use in Native
American populations is also high. Among the Lumbee
women in North Carolina, for instance, the use of
smokeless tobacco was discovered to be thirty-eight times
that for women in the total U.S. population in 1991.[11]
In addition to the fact that the local economy is based
largely on the tobacco crop, it is possible there are other
cultural factors behind the high rate of tobacco usage.
Tobacco has been used for medicinal purposes among
Native Americans for hundreds of years.

Higher rates of tobacco-related disease are exhibited
in some minority groups, especially among Native
Americans, a factor linked to increased smoking in this
group.

Interestingly, statistics from the CDC show that both
Hispanics and Asians living in the United States are less
likely to smoke than people from other ethnic groups in
this country. Reasons for this are not fully understood,
but some evidence suggests family pressures to avoid or
stop smoking are especially important.

Smoking among people living below the poverty level
in the United States is markedly higher than it is among
groups of higher socioeconomic status. Some of this
increase may be attributable to generally lower levels of
educational achievement and also to certain cultural factors having to do with racial or ethnic background.

An obstacle to reducing tobacco use in economically
deprived areas is the frequent lack of adequate health care

personnel and facilities. Doctors, nurses, and other health professionals are an important source of information about the health hazards of tobacco use. In their absence, the personal information and advice from a respected professional—information and advice that often makes the difference in deciding to quit smoking—is usually lacking.

We have to tell our children the truth about the diseases caused by smoking. For too long we have sent conflicting messages to our children and then have acted surprised when they begin to smoke.[1]

—Dr. David A. Kessler,
former commissioner of the Food and Drug Administration

5

Prevention Efforts

Because 80 percent to 90 percent of regular smokers adopt the habit before their eighteenth birthday, it stands to reason that prevention strategies are most effectively aimed at youth. Just as there are many factors that influence the decision to begin smoking, prevention efforts must approach the problem of smoking from many different avenues.

Some of the most commonly cited elements of effective tobacco-use prevention plans are:

- comprehensive school-based health education and tobacco prevention programs;

- restricted access of minors to tobacco products;

- restricted tobacco advertising aimed at youth;

- counter-advertising aimed at youth to deglamorize smoking; and

- increased taxes on tobacco products.

School-based Programs

School-based programs are reported to be among the most effective means of preventing tobacco use among youth. Schools are effective places for prevention programs because they are able to reach all young people and because students are in an environment where they are accustomed to learning important life skills.

Even if school-based programs are effective only in *delaying* the onset of smoking among children and teens, they are still worthwhile, according to experts. Even a delay reduces the chances that a young person will become a regular smoker as an adult and diminishes the odds for developing lung cancer and other smoking-related diseases later in life.

In 1994, the Centers for Disease Control and Prevention (CDC) issued guidelines for school health programs to prevent tobacco use and addiction.[2] The guidelines were developed in partnership with many individual experts as well as the input of numerous health and education organizations, including the American Cancer Society, American Heart Association, American Lung Association, Indian Health Service, National School Boards Association, and the U.S. Department of Education.

The guidelines set out seven recommendations for schools to implement in order to prevent tobacco use among youth.

1. Develop and enforce a school policy on tobacco use. The policy should prohibit tobacco use by students; by all school staff, parents, and visitors on school property; in school vehicles; and at school-sponsored functions away from school property. Education about avoiding tobacco use should be provided to students, and assistance in quitting should be made available to students and staff who use tobacco. The policy should also prohibit tobacco advertising in school buildings, at school functions, and in school publications, such as student newspapers, athletic programs, and similar organizations. Representatives for students, parents, school staff, and school board members should participate in developing and implementing the policy.

2. Provide instruction about the short-term and long-term negative health and social consequences of tobacco use, social influences on tobacco use, peer norms regarding tobacco use, and refusal skills. Rather than just providing information about tobacco's harmful effects or attempting to frighten young people about the consequences of tobacco use, school programs should address the many psychosocial factors related to tobacco use. Students should receive instruction on the multiple undesirable aspects of smoking—from stained teeth to cancer—and understand that most adolescents do not smoke. The program should also help students to understand why some adolescents do smoke (to be accepted by peers, to appear mature, to assert independence, to cope with stress, and so on) and to develop better ways of attaining these goals. Developing students' refusal skills to help them identify and reject pro-tobacco messages from advertising, adults, and peers is important also.

3. Provide tobacco-use prevention education in kindergarten through twelfth grade. This instruction should be especially intensive in junior high or middle school and should be reinforced in high school. Even basic concepts, such as "tobacco use is harmful to health" and "many people who use tobacco have trouble stopping," can be introduced in early elementary school.

Because tobacco use often begins in grades six through eight, it is recommended that prevention education be especially focused on these grades. "Particularly important is the year of entry into junior high or middle school when new students are exposed to older students who use tobacco at higher rates,"[3] advises the CDC document. Annual tobacco prevention education should be provided throughout high school to reinforce the concepts learned earlier and guard against older adolescents taking up the habit.

4. Provide adequate tobacco-use prevention training for teachers. Teachers need to have a thorough understanding of tobacco-use prevention techniques and know how to integrate such programs into their teaching.

5. Involve parents or families in support of school-based programs to prevent tobacco use. Parents and families provide important support to programs. In addition, the school-based program may provide additional motivation for adult smokers to quit.

6. Support cessation efforts among students and all school staff who use tobacco. Programs to help young people stop smoking are often unavailable within the community. If this is the case, schools should consider sponsoring such programs in coordination with existing community health agencies.

7. Assess the tobacco-use prevention program at regular intervals. School boards and school administrators should evaluate their programs to ensure that they are effective and in compliance with local and state policies.

Life Skills Training. A program called Life Skills Training, developed by the National Institute on Drug Abuse (NIDA), has reportedly been effective in preventing tobacco and other drug use by teenagers over a sustained period of time. Life Skills Training combines training in the skills and knowledge to resist social pressure to use tobacco products and other drugs with education in basic interpersonal skills and accurate information about the rate of tobacco and drug use.

The NIDA program developers concluded that an effective school-based prevention program for young teenagers must include a wide range of interpersonal skills, including building self-esteem, developing personal relationships, managing anxiety, and resisting social pressure. Such a program must also begin in junior high and include at least two years of booster sessions to be effective, they said. The Life Skills Training program consists of fifteen classes beginning in seventh grade, followed by ten booster sessions in eighth grade and five booster sessions in ninth grade.

The Life Skills results "provide the first evidence that a school-based intervention conducted by regular classroom teachers can produce reductions in tobacco, alcohol, and marijuana use that lasts through the end of high school," according to NIDA researchers.[4]

Another school-based tobacco-use prevention program is called the Smoke-Free Class of 2000, a joint

Many authorities support teaching children as young as five years old about the dangers of tobacco use.

effort of the American Cancer Society, the American Heart Association, and the American Lung Association. This program focuses on children who entered first grade in 1988 and will graduate from high school in the year 2000. Subsequent classes will also benefit from the materials developed for this project.

During the 1994–95 school year, the Smoke-Free Class of 2000 was in the seventh grade. A variety of educational materials were developed specifically for students at this age of development, including a ten-minute video showing teens learning about tobacco issues and working to help develop local smoking policies.

The Smoke-Free Class of 2000 also sponsored a letter-writing campaign in the 1994–95 school year. This program encouraged seventh-grade students to research a tobacco-related issue and write a letter concerning that topic to a local, state, or federal official. The authors of the two top letters from each state were rewarded with an all-expense paid trip to Washington, D.C., for a forum on tobacco issues. These and other activities throughout the year helped the students learn about tobacco topics and also enabled them to participate in developing smoking policies at their local level.

Restricted Access of Minors to Tobacco Products

As noted earlier in this book, state laws prohibit stores from selling tobacco products to people under eighteen. However, these so-called youth access laws are unevenly enforced. In fact, the federal government acknowledges that such laws are routinely ignored.

Strengthening youth access laws is the foundation of the restrictions announced by President Bill Clinton in 1996 and is a major component of the proposed settlement between tobacco companies and the state attorneys-general. Efforts to curb youth access include the ban on vending machines and self-service displays in areas to which people under eighteen have access. The rules would also prohibit the distribution of free tobacco products and single-cigarette sales.

Vending machines have been an important source of cigarettes for minors because most machines are not actively monitored by an adult. This is especially true for younger adolescents who are most likely to be turned away by a merchant.

In addition to recommendations that cigarette vending machines be outlawed entirely, there have been various attempts to limit access to the machines by placing them behind counters or in other restricted locations. Some machines have been modified to accept only special tokens, while others are equipped with electronic locking devices that require the store owner to supervise the sale. Despite these attempts to limit access, until now vending machines have remained an easy access point for youngsters.

Another source of tobacco for youngsters has been tobacco company giveaways. Historically, manufacturers have provided free cigarette samples as a way of introducing new products or advertising existing products to smokers. It also has been relatively easy for underage smokers to participate in these giveaways, either by intercepting mailed packages intended for someone else or by passing themselves off as an adult to an attendant distributing samples.

President Clinton also banned single-cigarette, or so-called loosie, sales, which were another way for minors to get tobacco. While such sales were not legal, some unscrupulous merchants were known to sell individual cigarettes to minors. In this way, a young person who might be unable to afford a full pack of cigarettes could gain access to one or two cigarettes at a time.

The suggestion that retailers be licensed to sell tobacco has gained significant support in recent years. The idea here is to give the state an additional enforcement mechanism: If a merchant is found to be selling tobacco products to minors, the required license could be suspended or revoked.

Tobacco Advertising

One of the most hotly debated areas of tobacco policy in recent years has been advertising. Both the initiation of the R.J. Reynolds Joe Camel campaign and the increasing emphasis on promotional products bearing tobacco brand names and logos have prompted calls for stricter regulation of tobacco advertising, especially that which is perceived to be aimed at young people.

The regulations announced by President Clinton were largely a response to such calls. While tobacco advertising is not completely banned under the new regulations, it is severely restricted. The measures, including limits on the types and locations of cigarette advertising, are designed to "decrease the positive imagery that makes these products appealing to children and adolescents."[5] Even stricter limitations on advertising could be seen if the 1997 settlement between tobacco companies and the state attorneys-general is enacted.

Beyond restrictions on tobacco company advertising and promotion, counter-advertising has been attempted in some regions. President Clinton instructed the FDA to make the cigarette industry initiate an advertising campaign about smoking hazards and the 1997 proposed settlement would further this effort. Also, as mentioned earlier in this book, states such as Massachusetts have launched their own series of antismoking ads. The intention of such efforts is to provide some challenge to the pro-tobacco messages and images youth are exposed to on an ongoing basis. Of course, in the past, the budget for such antismoking ads has never approached the $6 billion the tobacco industry spends every year to promote its products.

Increased Tobacco Taxes

Of all the prevention strategies routinely discussed, higher taxes on tobacco are believed by public health experts to be among the most effective in deterring youth smoking. More than other age groups, children and teens are highly sensitive to pricing. Therefore, efforts to raise the cost of smoking would most likely affect them first and foremost.

A 1994 report by the Institute of Medicine (IOM) recommended a two-dollar increase in the federal excise tax on cigarettes and similar increases on smokeless tobacco products. This and many other similar proposals have been offered with prevention efforts in mind. In recent years, some individuals and organizations have called for the use of a different tactic—raising tobacco taxes to help fund the cost of providing health care to uninsured Americans or to establish a fund to pay for the cost of providing medical care to people with smoking-related diseases.

"A $2 increase in the price would definitely stop a lot of teens from smoking," said one teen, quoted in the IOM report. "Kids have better ways to spend $5 than on cigarettes. A 50-cent increase wouldn't make any difference."[6]

The biggest mistake smokers/tobacco chewers make when trying to quit is giving up. Did you start smoking or chewing tobacco in only one attempt? Very few people succeed at complicated tasks the very first time. The same is true of people trying to stop using tobacco. The bottom line is KEEP TRYING.[1]

—Marlene M. Maheu, Ph.D.,
director, Nicotine Recovery Institute, San Diego, California

6

Treatment Options

With all of the information about the negative health effects of smoking, people who smoke for a long period of time may begin to assume that their fate is sealed. Fortunately, there are always more good reasons to quit than there are reasons to continue smoking.

Some health benefits of stopping smoking are immediate, including improved sense of taste and smell, better oral health, and lower carbon monoxide levels in the bloodstream. The economic benefits of quitting add up quickly, too. Some of the longer-term health benefits of stopping smoking are described below:

• After one year of cessation, smokers' excess risk of heart disease is reduced by half. After fifteen years of abstinence from smoking, the risk is similar to that of people who have never smoked.

- After ten years, the risk of lung cancer for former smokers falls to as much as half that of people continuing to smoke. The risk continues to decline with each additional smoke-free year.

- After fifteen years, the risk of death for former smokers is about the same as that of persons who have never smoked.

- Women who stop smoking before becoming pregnant or during the first trimester of pregnancy reduce their risk of having a low-birth-weight baby to that of women who have never smoked.[2]

According to the U.S. Surgeon General, nicotine is an addictive drug comparable to heroin and cocaine. Not surprisingly, therefore, a majority of cigarette smokers and other users of tobacco products are believed to suffer at least some level of nicotine addiction. This addiction, which involves both physical and psychological dependence, is strong and prevents many people who would like to stop smoking from doing so.

Studies show that most smokers' attempts to stop smoking are short-lived. In fact, less than half of all attempts to quit smoking cigarettes last even one week. Only about a quarter last one month. Relapse can occur for many years after a former smoker has quit.

Like users of other addictive drugs, people who try to stop smoking experience withdrawal symptoms. Anxiety, irritability, hunger, restlessness, lack of concentration, intense cravings for nicotine, drowsiness, and sleep disturbance are some of the various symptoms of nicotine withdrawal. Such symptoms are usually most pronounced in the first few days and weeks of abstinence.

In recent years, as smoking has increasingly been understood as an addictive behavior, cessation strategies have been developed or modified from existing drug treatment programs. Some strategies involve group programming, but while these have demonstrated some useful components, the vast majority of all smokers in the United States who have quit—more than 40 million people—have done so on their own.

Regardless of how one approaches the challenge of stopping smoking—in a group program or individually—the bottom line remains the same: Quitting is like a game of one-on-one. Each individual smoker must make the decision to quit for himself or herself. Each smoker must face the difficult consequences of addiction.

Nicotine Replacement Therapy

Because many of the withdrawal symptoms mentioned above are believed to stem from a smoker's dependence on nicotine, some products have been developed to administer doses of nicotine without the harmful side effects of cigarette smoke. These products are intended to help smokers cope with the physical withdrawal symptoms and concentrate more fully on the behavioral aspects of smoking cessation.

Two of the products used in so-called nicotine replacement therapy are nicotine gum and the nicotine patch. In general, both of these products, which are prescribed by physicians, are intended to assist the smoker who is highly nicotine dependent (smokes more than twenty-five cigarettes per day).

Nicotine gum became available in the United States

in the mid-1980s. Patients who chew it absorb nicotine through the lining of the mouth. Unfortunately, nicotine gum has demonstrated only limited success. Many users of the gum are not adequately instructed in its proper use, and, therefore, underdosing is a common problem.

In 1992, the nicotine patch was introduced and quickly replaced gum as the preferred product for use in nicotine replacement therapy. The patch is applied to the skin and gradually releases a controlled amount of nicotine into the blood supply. The dosage of these patches varies, with the highest-dose varieties providing nicotine levels of about half the amount observed in moderate to heavy smokers.

The nicotine patch is thought to have two primary advantages over gum: it is easier to use because the patient only needs to apply it once per day and it introduces a steady supply of nicotine into the bloodstream, which is preferable to the "jolt-of-nicotine" approach.

Initial results with the nicotine patch raised hopes that it would be extremely useful in smoking cessation efforts. Closely controlled studies showed the quit rates of patch users were about twice as high as their nonpatch counterparts. More recently, however, it has become clear that the patch is probably most effective when used in combination with other forms of cessation assistance, such as advice from a physician to stop smoking, enrollment in a behavior modification program, or even reading literature on how to successfully stop smoking.

Nicotine replacement therapy is not for everyone. Pregnant women, nursing mothers, and people with serious heart problems cannot use these products safely. In addition, those using the patch may experience certain undesirable side effects such as skin irritation, sweating, insomnia, and diarrhea, among others.

Some controversies remain over the use of nicotine replacement therapy. Some people suggest that products such as nicotine gum or nicotine patches are simply addictive substitutes themselves and should not be prescribed by physicians. There is also concern about the negative health effects of continued smoking while using nicotine gum or the patch. Smoking while using these nicotine replacement products could lead to nicotine overdoses which, in turn, can lead to severe cardiovascular health problems, including heart attacks.

The Quitting Process

As noted above, most ex-smokers have managed to stop smoking on their own, without the assistance of a formal cessation program. Even those who do use the services of a specific program find out that the most important part of the quitting process is self-guided, that is, it comes down to their own determination and effort to overcome the urge to smoke.

Regardless of whether a person approaches the task of stopping smoking individually or as part of a larger group, there are certain stages that every smoker passes through on the way to becoming smoke free. Smoking researchers have identified these motivational stages of quitting (see Table 1 on page 99) as a way to help individuals and program planners choose appropriate strategies in the battle against tobacco use. Because successful cessation often requires multiple attempts, the stages outlined in Table 1 should be viewed as cyclical. The goal is for

Table 1.
Stages of Quitting

Precontemplation   (Not yet considering quitting)

Contemplation   (Thinking about quitting)

Action   (Making a quit attempt)

Maintenance   (Remaining a nonsmoker)

Relapse   (Starting to smoke again)

Adapted from J. O. Prochaska and C. C. DiClemente, 1983.

smokers to always advance to the next stage of the quitting process, until they are able to quit for good.

Another important element in the quitting process is the larger environment of which smokers are a part. If smokers are constantly confronted with "cues"—objects or situations that remind them of their tobacco-use habit or allow them to partake in their habit—the odds of successfully quitting diminish. On the other hand, if the environment of a smoker who is trying to quit is filled with cues that support quitting efforts, the odds of success increase.

The public health community supports a wide variety of initiatives to help smokers achieve their cessation goals. Some examples of these environmental cues are shown in Table 2 on page 101.

Finally, there are many specific approaches that smokers can employ to break the tobacco-use habit. Because of the individual motivations for smoking as well as the individual features of the smoking habit itself, the quitting process varies from one smoker to the next. Some common themes and strategies for cessation attempts that are more likely to result in success appear in Quit Tips for Smokers on page 107. While the tips outlined there will not necessarily apply to every smoker trying to quit, many of them may be useful.

Common Errors

Quitting smoking is difficult and most people who try to do so will not succeed on their first attempt. Setbacks are nothing to be ashamed of, however. The main thing is for smokers to continue trying to quit and for their friends and family to remain supportive of their efforts.

Table 2.
Influences to Help Smokers Quit

- Smoking restrictions in public places, including schools, work sites, restaurants, and community hospitals.

- Smoking policies for meetings and facilities of community, social, and religious organizations.

- Nonsmoking public service announcements on radio and TV

- Nonsmoking campaigns carried out through work sites.

- Newspaper coverage of topics such as nonsmoking legislation, recent findings on health effects, the cost of smoking, or community smoking control efforts.

- Smoking and health messages on items such as grocery bags, billboards, or newsletters.

- Self-guided cessation programs published over several days in newspapers or shown on TV.

- Routine smoking status inquiry and brief counseling encouraging smokers to stop, provided by a variety of health professionals.

Adapted from the National Cancer Institute, 1990.

Smokers struggling to quit can help themselves by avoiding some frequent pitfalls. The following list of common errors is adapted from a list developed by Dr. Marlene Maheu, director of the Nicotine Recovery Institute in San Diego, California.

- Jumping in without a plan. Giving up cigarettes on a whim is a recipe for almost certain failure. Explore all of the quitting techniques available to you and then devise a concrete plan. Several options exist, such as self-help groups, relaxation exercises, and nicotine replacement therapy. Ask successful quitters what worked for them. Ask your doctor, too.

- Ignoring your uniqueness. Do you smoke as a social prop? To reduce stress? To control weight? Once you understand what causes you to light up, you can begin to explore other, less destructive ways to satisfy your needs.

- Quitting in secret. Smokers trying to quit often keep their intentions to themselves—just when they need allies most. Better: Don't worry about public failure or ridicule. Ask family, friends, and other students for support. Explain that you may be irritable for a while. Ask for patience, and no teasing.

- Believing you can have "just one." The only way to quit is to give up completely. For smokers, like alcoholics, a seemingly minor slip is inevitably followed by a relapse. During the first days and weeks after you quit, the urge to smoke may prove overwhelming at parties or with certain friends. If so, avoid them until your resolve not to smoke is stronger.[3]

Some smokers are convinced that they can gain health benefits by switching to a "low-tar" cigarette instead of quitting. In 1995, however, an expert advisory committee stated that the health benefits of such a switch are minimal compared to quitting smoking entirely.

"How you smoke may be more important than what you smoke," said Dr. Harold Freeman, chairman of the committee convened by Congress and the Federal Trade Commission (FTC).[4] Even with so-called low-tar cigarettes, smokers can modify their smoking behavior to increase their exposure to harmful compounds, including tar, nicotine, and carbon monoxide. For example, smokers may use their fingertips to cover up the tiny holes in the side of the cigarette filter, which are designed to pull in clean air and dilute the tobacco smoke inhaled into the lungs. Blocking off the holes prevents clean air from mixing with the smoke and thereby cancels out the supposed health benefits of a low-tar cigarette.

Another factor that discourages many smokers from quitting is a fear of weight gain. Some of these fears may be exaggerated. The 1990 Surgeon General's report on cigarette smoking reviewed 15 studies of weight gain following cessation. While about 80 percent of ex-smokers did put on some weight, the average gain was just five pounds. Such a nominal gain poses only minimal health risks—and such risks are far less than the health risks associated with continued smoking.

To minimize weight gain after quitting, ex-smokers should carefully monitor their diet and incorporate exercise into their lifestyle. Eating well-balanced meals that are low in fat, as well as consuming plenty of water, will provide protection against unnecessary weight gain after quitting.

The Simple Way to Avoid Quitting— Don't Start Smoking

The surest way to avoid the consequences of tobacco use and the difficulties of quitting is to not start smoking in the first place, health experts advise. However, as this book has discussed, tobacco use is entrenched in a large segment of the U.S. population and for these individuals, should they decide to quit, stopping will likely be quite difficult.

While it may not make the quitting process easier, acknowledging just how deeply tobacco issues have permeated the American culture can be instructive for both tobacco users and critics. Tobacco is a social issue, as demonstrated by the often contentious battles that pit smokers and nonsmokers against one another in schools, homes, workplaces, and public buildings. It is an economic issue involving a wide range of financial interests, from some of the wealthiest multinational corporations to small family farms that raise tobacco plants.

It is a political issue, as evidenced by the Clinton administration's decision to regulate some tobacco sales, advertising, and marketing, and the heated debate this initiative has sparked in legislative arenas nationwide.

Most importantly, perhaps, it is a health issue, with dire consequences for individuals who choose to smoke as well as for those who share their immediate environment.

As these and other aspects of the smoking issue unfold in the years ahead, Americans will confront complex questions involving individual rights, the fair treatment of both smokers and nonsmokers, the interests of business, and the physical well-being of everyone, especially children and young people. The ways we address these difficult issues will become yet another chapter in the story of tobacco in America.

Quit Tips for Smokers

1. Tips for Preparing to Stop

- Decide positively that you want to stop. Try to avoid negative thoughts about possible difficulties. The thoughts can be much worse than the experience of stopping itself.

- List all the reasons why you want to stop. Every night before going to bed, repeat one of the reasons ten times.

- Develop strong personalized reasons for stopping. For example, think of all the money you spend on cigarettes, or the strong odor tobacco smoke leaves on your hair and clothes.

- Begin to condition yourself physically: Start a modest exercise program, drink more fluids, get plenty of rest, and avoid fatigue.

- Know what to expect:
  - *Have realistic expectations—stopping isn't easy, but it's not impossible either. More than 3 million people in the United States stop every year.
  - *Understand that withdrawal symptoms are temporary and are healthy signs that the body is repairing itself from its long exposure to nicotine. Within twenty-four hours of stopping, withdrawal symptoms may appear as the body begins its healing process.

*Know that most relapses occur in the first week or two after stopping. At this time, withdrawal symptoms are strongest, and your body is still most dependent on nicotine. Be aware that this will be your most difficult time. Fully use all your personal resources—willpower, family, friends, and any tips that work for you—to get through this critical period successfully.

• Involve someone else:

*Bet a friend you can stop on your target date. Put your tobacco money aside every day, and forfeit it if you smoke or chew. (But if you do, don't give up; simply strengthen your resolve and try again.)

*Ask a friend or relative to stop with you. Make a "buddy" system to help you both follow through.

*Tell your family and friends that you're stopping and when. They can be an important source of support both before and after you stop.

2. Tips for Just Before Stopping

• Practice going without tobacco.

• Don't dwell on the fact that you will never use tobacco again. Think of being tobacco-free in terms of one day at a time.

- Stop carrying tobacco with you at all times. Make obtaining it difficult.

- Don't empty your ashtrays or the container that you spit into. This will remind you how much you have used each day, and the sight and smell will be very unpleasant.

- Collect all your cigarette butts into one large glass container as a visual reminder of the mess that smoking represents. Occasionally unscrew the lid to smell the foul butt and ash odors as a reminder of your former environment.

3. Tips for the Day You Stop

- Throw away all of your tobacco, lighters, ashtrays, spittoons, and other tobacco-related paraphernalia.

- Clean all of your clothes to rid them of the smell of smoke, which can linger a long time.

- Develop a clean, smoke-free environment around yourself—at school and at home. Buy yourself flowers—you may be surprised how much you can enjoy their scent now.

- Schedule an appointment to have your teeth cleaned. Resolve to keep them free of stains and preserve the feeling of a clean mouth.

- Make a list of things you'd like to buy for yourself or someone else. Estimate your cost of using tobacco and put the money aside to buy yourself a present.

- Keep very busy on the big day. Go to the movies, exercise, take long walks, or go bike riding.

- Buy yourself a treat or do something to celebrate.

- Stay away from other tobacco users as they could weaken your resolve (this need be only a temporary measure).

- Remember that one cigarette or one chew could ruin an otherwise successful attempt.

- Remember that alcohol will weaken your willpower. Avoid it.

- Refuse to allow anything to change your mind.

4. Tips to Help You Cope with the Periodic Urge to Use Tobacco

- First, remind yourself that you've stopped and you're a nonuser. Then, look closely at your urge to use tobacco and ask yourself:

  *Where was I when I got the urge?

  *What was I doing at the time?

  *Who was I with?

  *What was I thinking?

- Think about why you stopped:

  *Repeat to yourself (aloud if you're alone) your three main reasons for stopping.

  *Write down your three main reasons for stopping, then three reasons for not stopping.

110

• Anticipate triggers and prepare to avoid them:

* Keep your hands busy—doodle, knit, toss a football with friends.

* Avoid people who smoke or chew; spend more time with friends who do not use tobacco.

* Find activities that make smoking difficult (exercise, sleeping, washing the car, gardening, taking a shower).

* Put something other than tobacco in your mouth. Keep oral substitutes handy—try carrots, sunflower seeds, apples, celery, or sugarless gum instead. Use a mouthwash.

* Change your surroundings when an urge hits; get up and move around or do something else.

* Avoid places where smoking is permitted. Sit in the nonsmoking section in public places.

* Be prepared for "first times" as a nonuser: your first vacation, first time home alone, first long car ride, first period of boredom. If you know you will be in a high-risk situation, plan or rehearse how you will get through it without using tobacco.

• Change your daily routine to break your old habits and patterns:

* After meals, immediately get up from the table; brush your teeth or take a walk.

111

*Change the order in which you do things, particularly your morning routine.

*Don't sit in your favorite chair.

*Eat your lunch in a different location.

• Use positive thoughts:

*If self-defeating thoughts start to creep in, remind yourself again that you're a nonuser, that you don't want to be a user, and that you have good reasons for it.

*Make daydreaming work for you. For example, start planning a perfect vacation; work on that plan when thoughts about tobacco start to give you trouble.

*Look around you at all the people who do not smoke, including children. Remind yourself that they feel normal and healthy without using tobacco and so can you.

• Use relaxation techniques:

*Breathe in deeply and slowly, while you count to five; breathe out slowly, counting to five again.

*Take ten deep breaths and hold the last one while lighting a match. Exhale slowly and blow out the match. Pretend it is a cigarette, and crush it out in an ashtray.

5. Tips for Coping with Relapse

• Stop using tobacco immediately.

- Get rid of any tobacco products that you may have.

- Recognize that you've had a slip. A slip means you've had a small setback. But your first use of tobacco didn't make you a smoker or chewer to start with, and a small setback doesn't make you a smoker or chewer again.

- Don't be too hard on yourself. One slip doesn't mean you're a failure or that you can't be a nonuser, but it is important to get yourself back on the nonuser track immediately.

- Realize that many successful former tobacco users stop for good only after more than one attempt.

- Identify triggers: Exactly what was it that prompted you to use tobacco? Be aware of your triggers and decide now how you'll cope with them when they come up again.

- Sign a contract with yourself to remain a nonuser.

Adapted from the National Cancer Institute, 1990.

Where to Find Help

Alliance for Smoke-Free Air
P.O. Box 346
Old Bethpage, NY 11804
516-433-8278

American Cancer Society
1599 Clifton Road N.E.
Atlanta, GA 30329
1-800-ACS-2345

American Cancer Society Smoker Quitline
95 Berkeley Street
Boston, MA 02116
617-338-6018

American Lung Association
1740 Broadway
New York, NY 10019-4374
212-315-8700
1-800-LUNG-USA

American Nonsmokers Association
32 Glenwood Avenue
Newton, MA 02159

Americans for a Smoke-Free Society
2175 Lenox Road N.E., Suite A-7
Atlanta, GA 30324
404-299-2604

California Nicotine Anonymous
P.O. Box 25335
Los Angeles, CA 90025
1-800-642-0666 (CA only)

Citizens for a Tobacco-Free Society
8660 Lynnehaven Drive
Cincinnati, OH 45236-1420
513-677-6666

Fresh Air for Nonsmokers
P.O. Box 24052
Seattle, WA 98124
206-282-5565

Group Against Smoking Pollution (GASP)
7 Mazine Avenue
Plainview, NY 11803
516-938-0080

National Cancer Institute
Building 31, Room 10A24
Bethesda, MD 20892
1-800-492-6600
1-800-4-CANCER

National Center for Tobacco-Free Kids
1707 L Street, N.W., Suite 400
Washington, DC 20036
1-800-284-KIDS

National Clearinghouse on Tobacco and Health
1000 - 170 Laurier Avenue West
Ottawa, Ontario, K1P 5V5, Canada
613-567-3050

Nicotine Anonymous World Services
P.O. Box 591777
San Francisco, CA 94159-1777
415-750-0328

Office on Smoking and Health at the Centers for Disease Control
Mail Stop K-50
4770 Buford Highway, N.E.
Atlanta, GA 30341-3724
1-800-CDC-1311

Please No Smoking Club
P.O. Box 25972
Albuquerque, NM 87125
505-892-0291

Smoke Free Seminars
4932 Monroeville Road
Fort Wayne, IN 46836
219-639-3916

Stop Teenage Addiction to Tobacco
511 E. Columbus Ave.
Springfield, MA 01105
413-732-STAT

U.S. Environmental Protection Agency/Indoor Air Quality Information Clearinghouse
P.O. Box 37122
Washington, DC 20013-7133
1-800-438-4318

Chapter Notes

Chapter 1

1. *Preventing Tobacco Use Among Young People—A Report of the U.S. Surgeon General,* executive summary, U.S. Department of Health and Human Services, Atlanta, Ga., 1994, p.1.

2. Ibid., p. 5.

3. John Schwartz and Saundra Torry, "Tobacco Pact Calls for Strict Controls," *Washington Post,* June 21, 1997, p. A1; John M. Broder, "Cigarette Makers Reach $368 Billion Accord," *The New York Times,* p. A1.

Chapter 2

1. *Children and Tobacco: The Problem,* fact sheet, U.S. Food and Drug Administration, Rockville, Md., 1995.

2. *The Surgeon General's Report for Kids About Smoking,* U.S. Department of Health and Human Services, Atlanta, Ga., 1994.

3. *Preventing Tobacco Use Among Young People: A Report of the Surgeon General,* executive summary, U.S. Department of Health and Human Services, Atlanta, Ga., 1994, p. 6.

4. "Special Communications," *Journal of the American Medical Association,* July 19, 1995.

5. *Tobacco and the Clinician,* National Institutes of Health, Bethesda, Md., January 1994, p. iii.

6. "Gone Are the Days When Tobacco Brought Only Wealth," *The New York Times,* February 26, 1995.

7. "Business Week 1000," *Business Week,* March 27, 1995.

8. "Executive Pay," *Wall Street Journal,* April 12, 1995.

9. "The Inhalers," *Common Cause Magazine,* Spring 1995.

10. "Tobacco Industry Impacts Balance of Power in the California Legislature," UCSF News Release, May 23, 1995.

11. Richard Corliss, "What's All the Fuming About?" *Time*, April 18, 1994.

12. "Recordbreaking Sales," *Tobacco Reporter*, March 1995.

13. "U.S. Cigarette Production Rose 10% to 726 Billion Cigarettes in 1994," Dow Jones News Service, April 5, 1995.

14. Ibid.

15. "Survey of Attitudes Toward Smoking," *American Lung Association News*, December 5, 1985.

16. *Tobacco or Health: Status in the Americas*, Pan American Health Organization, 1992.

17. D. Satcher and M. Eriksen, "The Paradox of Tobacco Control," editorial, *Journal of the American Medical Association*, vol. 271, 1994, pp. 627–628.

18. *Children and Tobacco: The Problem.*

19. *The Surgeon General's Report for Kids About Smoking.*

20. Ibid.

21. Ibid.

22. "Racetrack Watch Moves on Tobacco," *Raleigh News and Observer*, April 16, 1995.

23. "Generic Cigarettes Exploit Advertising Loopholes," *Journal of the National Cancer Institute*, April 19, 1995.

24. *Domestic Cigarette Advertising and Promotional Expenditures*, U.S. Federal Trade Commission, Washington, D.C., May 2, 1995.

25. *Tobacco: Helping Youth Say No*, Tobacco Institute and the Family C.O.U.R.S.E. Consortium, 1991, p. 9.

26. *Preventing Tobacco Use Among Young People*, p. 8.

27. Ibid., p. 7.

28. Ibid.

29. *Tobacco*, fact sheet, American Medical Association, Chicago, Ill., June 1994.

30. "Cigarettes," editorial, *Detroit Free Press*, April 19, 1994.

31. *The Health Consequences of Smoking: Nicotine Addiction*, a report of the Surgeon General, U.S. Department of Health and Human Services, Atlanta, Ga., 1988.

32. *Preventing Tobacco Use Among Young People*, p. 6.

33. David A. Kessler's statement on nicotine-containing cigarettes, presented to the Subcommittee on Health and the Environment, Committee on Energy and Commerce, U.S. House of Representatives, March 25, 1994.

34. Ibid.

Chapter 3

1. *School Programs to Prevent Smoking*, National Cancer Institute, January 1990.

2. Centers for Disease Control and Prevention, "Medical-care Expenditures Attributable to Cigarette Smoking—United States, 1993," *Morbidity and Mortality Weekly Report*, July 8, 1994.

3. Joseph Califano's testimony before the Senate Finance Committee, March 10, 1994.

4. *Facts About the National Cancer Program*, National Cancer Institute, November 1994.

5. *Cancer Facts and Figures*, American Cancer Society, Atlanta, Ga., 1994.

6. *Smoking and Cancer*, National Cancer Institute, March 1995.

7. *Study Links Smoking and Increased Risk of Fatal Breast Cancer*, American Cancer Society, Atlanta, Ga., May 15, 1994, (news release).

8. "Leader in Cancer War Looks Ahead," Medical News and Perspectives, *Journal of the American Medical Association*, February 15, 1995.

9. *Cigarettes Add a Decade's Worth of Thickening to Neck Arteries*, news release, American Heart Association, Dallas, Tx., December 15, 1994.

10. R. A. Windsor, "The Dissemination of Smoking Cessation Methods for Pregnant Women: Achieving the Year 2000 Objectives," *American Journal of Public Health*, vol. 83, 1993, pp. 173–178.

11. J. DiFranza and R. Lew, *Journal of Family Practice*, April 1995.

12. *The National Heart, Lung, and Blood Fact Book*, Fiscal Year 1994.

13. *Cancer Facts—Environmental Tobacco Smoke*, National Cancer Institute, April 1995.

14. *Court Rules Tobacco Interests Have Standing in Lawsuit Against the EPA*, R.J. Reynolds Tobacco Company, Winston-Salem, N.C., May 24, 1995.

15. Thomas J. Bliley's statement to the Subcommittee on Health and Environment, Committee on Energy and Commerce, U.S. House of Representatives, July 21, 1993.

16. American Heart Association, "Environmental tobacco smoke and cardiovascular disease. A position paper from the AHA Council on Cardiopulmonary and Critical Care," *Circulation*, vol. 86, 1992, p. 1.

17. *NSA Criticizes Maryland Smoking Ban; Predicts Devastating Impact on State Businesses*, National Smokers Alliance, Alexandria, Va., March 2, 1995.

18. *NSA Decries National Campaign to Ban Smoking in Private Residences*, news release, National Smokers Alliance, Sacramento, Calif., May 4, 1995.

19. S. A. Glantz and W. W. Parmley, "Passive Smoking and Heart Disease," *Journal of the American Medical Association*, vol. 273, 1995, p. 1047.

20. *Setting the Record Straight: Secondhand Smoke is a Preventable Health Risk*, Environmenal Protection Agency, Washington, D.C., June 1994.

21. Richard Corliss, "What's All the Fuming About?" *Time*, April 19, 1994.

Chapter 4

1. David A. Kessler's statement on the control and manipulation of nicotine in cigarettes, presented to the Subcommittee on Health and the Environment, Committee on Energy and Commerce, U.S. House of Representatives, June 21, 1994.

2. *Preventing Tobacco Use Among Young People: A Report of the Surgeon General,* executive summary, U.S. Department of Health and Human Services, Atlanta, Ga., 1994, p. 6.

3. *President Clinton Announces Historic Steps to Reduce Children's Use of Tobacco,* U.S. Food and Drug Administration, Rockville, Md., August 23, 1996.

4. *Preventing Tobacco Use Among Young People: A Report of the Surgeon General,* p. 7.

5. *Youth Access to Tobacco Survey,* RWJF, 1995.

6. *Risk Factors—Cigarette/Tobacco Smoke,* AHA fact sheet, 1994.

7. Centers for Disease Control and Prevention, "Indicators of Nicotine Addiction Among Women—United States, 1991-1992," *Morbidity and Mortality Weekly Report,* vol. 44, 1995, p. 102.

8. *Cancer Facts and Figures,* American Cancer Society, 1994.

9. E. R. Gritz, "Lung Cancer: Now, More than Ever, a Feminist Issue," CA 43:197, 1993.

10. Centers for Disease Control and Prevention, "Cigarette Smoking Among Adults—United States, 1992, *Morbidity and Mortality Weekly Report,* vol. 43, 1994, p. 342.

11. Centers for Disease Control and Prevention, "Smokeless Tobacco Use Among American Indian Women—Southeastern North Carolina, 1991," *Morbidity and Mortality Weekly Report,* vol. 44, 1995, p. 113.

Chapter 5

1. *President Clinton Announces Historic Steps to Reduce Children's Use of Tobacco,* U.S. Food and Drug Administration, Rockville, Md., August 23, 1996.

2. Centers for Disease Control and Prevention, "Guidelines for School Health Programs to Prevent Tobacco Use and Addiction," *Morbidity and Mortality Weekly Report,* February 25, 1994.

3. Ibid.

4. *School-based Prevention Program Reduces Teens' Drug Use Through the End of High School,* National Institute on Drug Abuse, April 11, 1995.

5. U.S. Food and Drug Administration, "Proposed Rule Restricting Sale of Tobacco Products to Children," *Journal of the American Medical Association,* October 11, 1995.

6. Institute of Medicine, "Growing Up Tobacco Free," 1994.

Chapter 6

1. Marlene M. Maheu, Ph.D., *Quitting Smoking: Common Errors,* San Diego, Calif., 1995 (brochure).

2. *Cessation and Quitting,* Action on Smoking and Health, Washington, D.C., 1995, (leaflet).

3. Maheu.

4. "New Low-Tar Cigarettes Pose Hidden Threat, Panel Says," *Journal of the National Cancer Institute,* January 4, 1995, p. 15.

Further Reading

The Major Health Hazards of Smoking to Smokers. Action on Smoking and Health.

Fact Sheet: Risk Factors—Cigarette/Tobacco Smoke. American Heart Association, 1994.

"Women and Smoking," editorial. *American Journal of Public Health,* vol. 83, 1993, p. 1202.

"Survey of Attitudes Toward Smoking." *American Lung Association News,* December 5, 1985.

American Medical Association Fact Sheet: Tobacco. June 1994.

"Business Week 1000." *Business Week,* March 27, 1995.

Gritz, ER. "Lung Cancer: Now, More Than Ever, a Feminist Issue." *CA,* vol. 43.

American Heart Association. "Environmental tobacco smoke and cardiovascular disease. A position paper from the AHA Council on Cardiopulmonary and Critical Care." *Circulation,* vol. 86, no. 1, 1992.

"The Inhalers." *Common Cause Magazine.* Spring 1995.

"Cigarettes," editorial. *Detroit Free Press,* April 19, 1994.

"U.S. Cigarette Production Rose 10% to $726 Billion Cigarettes in 1994." Dow Jones News Service. April 5, 1995.

Joseph Califano's testimony before the Senate Finance Committee, March 10, 1994.

DiFranza, J. and Lew, R. *Journal of Family Practice*, April 1995.

"From the Food and Drug Administration: Proposed Rule Resticting Sale of Tobacco Products to Children." *Journal of the American Medical Association*, vol. 274, 1995, p. 1109.

Satcher, D. and M. Eriksen. "The paradox of tobacco control," editorial. *Journal of the American Medical Association*, vol. 271, 1994, pp. 627–628.

Glantz, S.A. and W.W.Parmley. "Passive Smoking and Heart Disease." *Journal of the American Medical Association*, vol. 273, 1995, p. 1047.

"Leader in Cancer War Looks Ahead." Medical News and Perspectives. *Journal of the American Medical Association*, vol. 273, 1995, p. 525.

"Special Communications: The Brown and Williamson Documents." Series. *Journal of the American Medical Association*, vol. 274, 1995, pp. 219–258.

"Generic Cigarettes Exploit Advertising Loopholes." *Journal of the National Cancer Institute*, vol. 87, 1995, p. 566.

CDC: "Cigarette Smoking Among Adults—United States, 1992." *Morbidity and Mortality Weekly Report*, vol. 43, 1994, p. 342.

CDC: "Guidleines for School Health Programs to Prevent Tobacco Use and Addiction." *Morbidity and Mortality Weekly Report*, vol. 43, no. RR-2, p. 1.

CDC: "Indicators of Nicotine Addiction Among Women—United States, 1991–1992." *Morbidity and Mortality Weekly Report*, vol. 44, 1995, p. 102.

CDC: "Medical-care Expenditures Attributable to Cigarette Smoking—United States, 1993. *Morbidity and Mortality Weekly Report*, vol. 43, 1994, p. 469.

CDC: "Smokeless Tobacco Use Among American Indian Women—Southeastern North Carolina, 1991." *Morbidity and Mortality Weekly Report*, vol. 44, 1995, p. 113.

National Cancer Institute. *Cancer Facts—Environmental Tobacco Smoke.* April 1995.

National Cancer Institute. *Facts About the National Cancer Program.* November 1994.

National Cancer Institute. *School Programs to Prevent Smoking.* January 1990.

National Cancer Institute. *Smoking and Cancer.* March 1995.

National Institutes of Health. *Tobacco and the Clinician.* January 1994.

"Gone Are the Days When Tobacco Brought Only Wealth." *The New York Times*, February 26, 1995.

Pan American Health Organization. *Tobacco or Health: Status in the Americas.* 1992.

"Racetracks Watch Moves on Tobacco." *Raleigh News & Observer*, April 16, 1995.

Robert Wood Johnson Foundation. *Youth Access to Tobacco Survey.* 1995.

SGR 4 Kids, The Surgeon General's Report for Kids About Smoking, 1994.

The National Heart, Lung, and Blood Fact Book, Fiscal Year 1994.

Richard Corliss. "What's All the Fuming About?" *Time*, April 19, 1994.

Record Breaking Sales. Tobacco Reporter. March 1995.

The Health Consequences of Smoking: Nicotine Addiction. A Report of the Surgeon General, 1988. U.S. Department of Health and Human Services.

Preventing Tobacco Use among Young People. A Report of the Surgeon General, 1994. U.S. Department of Health and Human Services.

Setting the Record Straight: Secondhand Smoke Is a Preventable Health Risk. U.S. Environmental Protection Agency, June 1994.

Domestic Cigarette Advertising and Promotional Expenditures. U.S. Federal Trade Commission, May 2, 1995.

Children and Tobacco: The Problem. U.S. Food and Drug Administration, 1995.

Tobacco Industry Impacts Balance of Power in the California Legislature, According to UCSF Analysis. UCSF News Release, May 23, 1995.

"Executive pay." *Wall Street Journal.* April 12, 1995.

"Growing Up Tobacco Free." Institute of Medicine, 1994.

Index